No Friend Like a Sister

No Friend Like a Sister

A Celebration in Words and Memories

Barbara Alpert

BERKLEY BOOKS, NEW YORK

A listing of additional sources, credits, and permissions appears at the back of this book.

NO FRIEND LIKE A SISTER

A Berkley Book / published by arrangement with
the author

ISBN: 0-425-15531-5

BERKLEY®
Berkley Books are published by The Berkley Publishing Group,
200 Madison Avenue, New York, New York 10016.
BERKLEY and the "B" design
are trademarks belonging to Berkley Publishing Corporation.

PRINTED IN THE UNITED STATES OF AMERICA

*For my parents, who inspire and encourage me, and
for the friends who have been like sisters to me*

Introduction

What is a sister?

She is your mirror, shining back at you with a world of possibilities. She is your witness, who sees you at your worst and best, and loves you anyway. She is your partner in crime, your midnight companion, someone who knows when you're smiling, even in the dark. She is your teacher, your defense attorney, your personal press agent, even your shrink. Some days, she's the reason you wish you were an only child. But most of the time her very existence creates a sense of acceptance, of community, of tenderness that comforts you and strengthens your resolve to go on, to do better, to travel the unfamiliar borders of your soul.

When I first undertook this project, determined to explore the many facets of sisterly friendship, I was met with quizzical looks. "Why you?" people asked. "After all, *you* don't have a sister." It's true—I don't. But I wanted to know once and for all how it feels to *have* a sister—and how it feels to *be* a sister. I looked forward to spending time in the company of sisters whose warmth for each other spilled onto the printed page, much as it had in the books I had read as a child.

I've heard it said that you can't miss what you never had, but when it comes to the special bond of sisterhood, I've always wondered if having a sister might have changed my life in some way. I grew up in a houseful of boys, and while I treasured my independence and privacy, I sometimes wished for a sister to play with, a friend to whisper secrets to in the dark. And when I read *Little Women*, I understood instinctively that my heroine Jo March might never have become the writer and woman she did without the throng of loving sisters who surrounded her, encouraged her, acted in her plays, and shared her journey.

What began as curiosity has, over the years, developed into a kind of wonderful obsession, and this book reflects my fascination with the many roles that sisters play in women's lives. In so many instances, I was intrigued to observe how sisters provided a kind of safety net and support system for each other, especially during times when society did not welcome their efforts to succeed in new roles. As these sisters shared their hopes and longings in letters, confessed their feelings in journals and diaries, pursued their dreams as writers, artists, activists, and more, they came vividly to life—and touched me with their passion for living and their devotion to each other.

It can be difficult to spend time in the presence of loving sisters without feeling a little bit like an outsider, envious of the bond they share. But once you are invited to become a part of that special inner circle, their warmth and friendship for each other will envelop you as well. You may not, as they do, share a history or blood, but as you journey through the pages of this book, you will feel an extraordinary kinship.

Barbara Alpert

No Friend
Like a Sister

For there is no friend like a sister,
In calm or stormy weather,
To cheer over the tedious way,
To fetch one if one goes astray,
To lift one if one totters down,
To strengthen whilst one stands.

—*from* Goblin Market *by Christina Rossetti*

Last night Margot and I were lying side by side in my bed. It was incredibly cramped, but that's what made it fun. She asked if she could read my diary once in a while.

"Parts of it," I said, and asked about hers. She gave me permission to read her diary as well.

The conversation turned to the future, and I asked what she wanted to be when she was older. But she wouldn't say and was quite mysterious about it. I gathered it had something to do with teaching; of course, I'm not absolutely sure, but I suspect it's something along those lines. I really shouldn't be so nosy. . . .

I once asked Margot if she thought I was ugly. She said that I was cute and had nice eyes. A little vague, don't you think?

—Anne Frank writing about her sister Margot in her diary,
October 14, 1942

All week we had been in a state about what to wear. At the last minute I asked the maid to take in my white lace dress which she did by clutching two great handfuls and sewing them up. It was so tight Jackie had to wear it. She could only get into it sideways so she looked rather strange from the front. We had no dinner and spent the evening in a frenzy of getting ready. As we clumped out the door, me in a great yellow thing of Jackie's I kept tripping on, I moaned, "Oh, I don't even want to go." "Don't you ever want to meet fascinating people or just spend all your time with your dreary little American friends," exploded Jackie as we raced down the hall.

We stumbled up the stairs of 34 Rue de la Faisanderie after a harrowing taxi ride. . . . They were all still in the dining room still eating dinner! While 10 or 12 butlers were busy lighting chandeliers we tiptoed around the room too terrified to even smoke because we might dirty a Louis XVI ashtray.

Finally with a great roar the dining room doors burst open and they came towards us—a horde of Ambassadors, Dukes, Counts and Princes, and women with emerald necklaces clanging against their knees. They would only speak to someone if they were a notch above them so you can imagine how many spoke to us.

> —*Lee Bouvier (later Radziwill), age 17, recalling the night she and her sister Jackie (later Kennedy Onassis) attended a Paris soiree*

Neither one of us ever married and we've lived together most all of our lives, and probably know each other better than any two human beings on Earth. After so long, we are in some ways like one person. She is my right arm. If she were to die first, I'm not sure if I would want to go on living because the reason I am living is to keep *her* living.

—*Sadie (Sarah) Delany, age 103, writing about her sister, Bessie (Elizabeth), age 101, in* Having Our Say

Sun out this afternoon. Con and I took a walk over a hill—we looked back and saw yellow daisies against the sky, daisy heads bobbing against the sky. Con and I talked. If I *never* in my life meet anyone else, I have been happier than anyone who ever lived in knowing her. It must be like being in love. I am never envious of her—her writing, her music, anything. I know how wonderful she is. Nothing is too good for her. . . .

—*Anne Morrow (Lindbergh) writing in her diary about her sister Constance in June, 1928*

Elizabeth [seven years younger] became my delight. Mother became pregnant again very soon and my youngest sister Priscilla was born only eighteen months later. . . .

They were already beginning to show clear contrasts in temperament, which Grandma pointed out as she set me to work taking notes on their behavior—on the first words Priscilla spoke and on the way one echoed the other. She made me aware of how Priscilla mimicked the epithets and shouts hurled up and down the back stairs by the Swedish nurse and the Irish cook and of how Elizabeth was already making poetry of life. Told that her dress was ragged, she replied happily, "Yes, I's the raggedy man." I learned to make these notes with love, carrying on what Mother had begun. I knew that she had filled thirteen notebooks on me and only four on Richard; now I was taking over for the younger children. In many ways I thought of the babies as my children, whom I could observe and teach and cultivate. I also wanted to give them everything I had missed. This continued until, when they were eight and ten, I gave them both lockets and discovered that neither of them had ever wanted a locket.

—*Margaret Mead recalling her sisters Elizabeth and Priscilla*

An Epistle to Henrietta—14th May 1814

Thy gentle smile displays thy virtues sweet,
Altho' dear Addles far to [*sic*] much you eat,
But now you have a horrid cold,
And in an ugly night cap you are rolled,
Which spoils the nat'ral beauty of your face,
Where dimples play in every cunning place;
I wish you would so nicely run,
And then we would have merry fun,
But o'er the fire you poking sit,
As if for nothing you were fit.
Our little lamb is very well,
Oh come into our pretty cell!
Indeed I hope you'll soon get better,
And I am dearest Henrietta
Your very dear Elizabeth Barrett,
Compared to you, a chatting parot [*sic*].

> —*Elizabeth Barrett (later Browning), age 8, writing a get-well poem to her younger sister Henrietta*

To My Dearest Ba
on Her Birthday
March 6th 1824

No aid Apollo I need ask of thee.
Nor thou Minerva, thou e'er scorneth me,
Thy presence e'en today thou wilt not give
Although I write to one you so much love;
Yes she is loved by you, and that I know
On her, thy bounty doest e'er bestow;
But is she loved by none but you
Oh no, she's loved by *many many* too
And why? is it because to her thy aid is given
No, not that alone, for she is loved by Heaven,
Yes, she is good, I love her well,
How much I do, I feel, to you I need not tell—

May I be allowed to wish dearest Ba *most perfect* health and happiness for *many* years and may I flatter myself that I am her dearest Henrietta.

—*Henrietta Moulton-Barrett writing to her sister Elizabeth Barrett (later Browning) on her birthday*

We were friends throughout life, with that intimacy but also—as children—the squabbling that resulted from our sharing a bed for many years: our parents' discarded double bed, after they had become so modern as to acquire separate English iron beds. We usually made a "frontier" with sheet folds carefully separating our domains. 1918 saw the end of this intimacy that only existed in wintertime; during the summers we were gloriously free in the attic where we could make separate nests.

> —*Alva Myrdal, social reformer and feminist, writing about her younger sister Rut*

During my childhood, my older sister, Daryl, and I shared the back seat of our parents' white Chevrolet on weekend family outings— but an imaginary line divided the seat into separate, hostile camps. If Daryl's arm or leg strayed onto my turf, or vice versa, the car was immediately transformed into a battle zone, with bickering and shouting that even a game of States or Capitals couldn't silence.

But as clearly as I can recall these skirmishes, I can also remember quite different experiences with Daryl during these outings. Late at night, coming home from holiday dinners at our aunt's home just hours after one of our quarrels, my eyelids would become heavy and I'd snuggle next to Daryl and rest my head on her lap. The imaginary dividing line forgotten, she would gently stroke my hair and twirl my ponytail, and often I would feel so close to her that I'd try to fight off sleep to savor the moment. My big sister was taking care of me.

> —*Dale Atkins, Ph.D., writing about her sister Daryl*

My sister had a game which both fascinated and terrified me. This was "The Elder Sister." The theme was that in our family was an elder sister, senior to my sister and myself. She was mad and lived in a cave at Corbin's Head, but sometimes she came to the house. She was indistinguishable in appearance from my sister, except for her voice, which was quite different. It was a frightening voice, a soft oily voice.

"You know who I am, don't you, dear? I'm your sister Madge. You don't think I'm anyone else, do you? You wouldn't think *that?*"

I used to feel indescribable terror. Of course I really knew it was only Madge pretending—but was it? Wasn't it perhaps true? That voice—those crafty sideways glancing eyes. It *was* the elder sister!

My mother used to get angry. "I won't have you frightening the child with this silly game, Madge."

Madge would reply reasonably enough: "But she asks me to do it."

I did. I would say to her:

"Will the elder sister be coming soon?"

"I don't know. Do you want her to come?"

"Yes—yes, I do...."

Did I really? I suppose so.

My demand would never be satisfied at once. Perhaps two days later there would be a knock at the nursery door, and the voice:

"Can I come in, dear? It's your elder sister...."

Many, many years later, Madge had only to use the elder sister voice and I would feel chills down my spine.

—*Agatha Christie writing about her sister Madge*

I'm four years old, and my sister Sasha is nine months old. We share a room. I watch her so she doesn't fall or touch something she's not supposed to. I feed her rice—she likes rice—and she plays in my tent with me. I sing my favorite song, "Go, Go, Power Rangers," and I dance with her, rock 'n' roll dancing. I like to pick her up because she puts her head on my shoulder.

Being an older sister is a little hard, because sometimes she bites me—she has teeth now. But I can teach her some interesting stuff, like the ABCs and dancing. When she gets a little older, we can do more together.

I love Sasha and she loves me.

—*Zoe Stahl, New York City preschooler, on her baby sister Sasha*

Children are not produced essentially as gifts for each other; but since they come like gifts, unasked for, very often as surprises to the existing children, as something special to be kept and not broken and discarded, I suppose it is true to say that there is no gift which quite equals the gift of a sister born when you are fourteen months old and still holding a precious first place in the household. Even the displacement, which is bound to occur, provides a certain independence and an undisputed status, that of "the elder sister."

There came a time in my own life when it suddenly became clear to me that my sister was the one person who had known me for the longest time. With this realisation a number of thoughts followed. One was that the only person who has ever wanted to hear me sing is my sister. In all the things we have shared—earache, chickenpox, measles, sweets, toys, books, love, ambition, shame, fear, to name a few, our two voices have been the most consistently shared. . . .

—*Elizabeth Jolley, Australian essayist, writing about her sister*

When we were kids, Anna and I shared a room. You had to learn either to get along or not to, which normally produces sisters who are friends or who hate each other. Our parents didn't tolerate our going off on our own separate ways, so what happened was that Anna had to get a date for me when she went out with a guy, so that my mother knew we were keeping an eye on each other. We did that a while, but eventually we worked up the routine of "Look, I'll meet you back at the front door at one A.M."

—*Kate McGarrigle talking about her sister and singing partner,*
Anna

How do people make it through life without a sister? As an identical twin sister, I have a built-in best friend, and we've been inseparable since birth. I need her as much as she needs me. She is my biggest security in life. We live three doors down from each other, we work together, we share the same passions and hobbies, and we even fight like cats and dogs. Mary creates for me a sense of well-being beyond any relationship I have ever experienced. Without her, where would I be? It's a unique relationship. We share a soul. We live in a special space. We thrive on combined spirit.

Life is twice as nice with an identical twin sister.

—*Sara Corpening talking about her sister, Mary Barber, her partner*
in Thymes Two Catering, San Francisco

To Christina Rossetti's "No friend like a sister," let me add, "No kin like a twin!" The strength that I have absorbed through my twin has fueled me throughout my life, but as all sisters know, the hate can be as strong as that between two lovers . . . until it suddenly dissipates into thin air.

For the past two years, my sister and I have run a small business, Thymes Two Catering, and believe me, since we started working together, our life has been full of challenges, spiced with laughter and tears. I'll never forget one rainy afternoon during the holiday season. We had been up for days and sleepless nights, working ourselves into a state of oblivion. Cross-eyed with fatigue and one more party to go, we kept wondering how we were going to persevere. We just kept saying, "Thank God we have each other." Finally, we finished the Beef Bourguignonne and began packing the car. Together, using our combined strength, we lifted this overwhelmingly large crate full of food and slowly, tediously, began carrying it down the stairs. With no energy and a lazy step, I tripped and fell to the ground.

My ankle sore and my face splattered with milk, I looked to my sister for sympathy. Instead, she shouted, "Get up! We're late! You clutz!" Furious, I pulled myself from under the crate, cocked back my arm, and hurled my fist into her back with all the strength I could muster. She fell to the ground, and we both sat down and wept. It was the culmination of sheer exhaustion and a much-needed release of emotion. Not five minutes later, of course, we started laughing uproariously, and we did not stop until we got to the party.

> —*Mary Barber writing about her sister, Sara Corpening, her twin and partner in Thymes Two Catering, San Francisco*

Nellie wasn't listening. She was thinking of her early relationship with Augusta, so tender and exciting that it ran through her memory like a clear stream. A love affair, really.

Augusta would take Nellie around everywhere. They would sit in the shower stall, brown tiles all around. It was like being inside a tall box. Augusta would say they were orphans lost in the woods. She would fill the cavernous shower with images of trees and ferns, the water slurping and spilling off the leaves onto their skin. She would put a finger to her lips and whisper, It's a bear and we have to be still as glass because he is so near his breath ruffles up the bottom of the curtain and we can feel it on our legs. We are so wet and cold and we have to huddle together, but it's hard to hold on because our hands are soapy and they slip all over each other.

—*from* Wild Apples *by Lucinda Franks*

Cary had been closer to me than anyone else. She was the only one of my elder sisters who had cared for me when I was a child and Emily, Annie, and Cary were all grown girls, interested in love and lovers. After Mother's death, when I was rewriting *The Descendant*, she was the one person I confided in, and her sympathy and criticism were of inestimable value. I used to think that I could never write another line if I were to lose her. Yet it is one of my deepest regrets, and there are many, that she died before I was ready to do my best work . . . Even now, after so many years, the sharp pang of that regret will sometimes awaken me in the night. But, so long as Cary was with me, I read my manuscripts aloud to her, chapter by chapter, and we would discuss the characters as if they were actual persons. She had the most brilliant mind and personality I have ever known; yet she could fling her whole interest into something outside herself.

> —*Ellen Glasgow, Pulitzer Prize–winning novelist for* In This Our Life, *remembering her beloved sister Cary*

Shirley always believed I would make it someday, even when I didn't. She would come to any state she could to see whatever show I was doing. She would drive for six or seven hours to be there. And even when things were very bad, she never once said to me, "Look, why don't you give this up and get a real job?" For seventeen years, she kept the faith.

> —*Janet Hubert-Whitten, actress, recalling the unfailing support of her older sister Shirley*

My sister Wilma seemed, along with all her other qualities, to have a deeper spiritual nature than the rest of us and that was supposed to be good. Besides, when she entered Radcliffe in 1927, she suddenly took a great leap forward and left us far behind. She had some serious-minded boyfriends who talked about ideas and such deep subjects as their "philosophy of life," and some more light-hearted ones who took her to Lampoon dances. Our boyfriends, if we had any, might pass us "mash" notes under the teacher's eye, which of course we would never acknowledge as a matter of pride. . . .

The influence of my sister Wilma was strong, however, and there was a great deal of emphasis on being "intellectual" and having "intellectual conversations" with one's boyfriends. But having an "intellectual" boyfriend was not enough unless he had a "sense of humor," and a sense of humor was judged by whether he thought the "private jokes" that seemed inevitably to have developed in a closely knit family of girls were funny. As for "being intellectual," it was also subject to enigmatic interpretation. In my case, the name of the game seemed to be combat rather than content. Ideas were for fighting, intellectual exercise was a form of skirmish, and the summoning of argument for the final coup de grace was the supreme ambition. The idea that we should refrain from argument because our adversaries were male never entered our heads and we looked with contempt on any pusillanimous contemporaries who played dumb in their pursuit of their "boyfriends." If our beaus couldn't stand the heat and didn't like being routed by "superior brain power," they could lump it! And a lot of them did.

—*Marian Cannon Schlesinger, painter, on the inspiration provided by her older sister Wilma*

I have always loved my sister's voice. It is clear and light, a voice without seasons, like bells over a green city or snowfall on the roots of orchids. Her voice is a greening thing, an enemy of storm and dark and winter.

—*Tom Wingo, narrator of Pat Conroy's* The Prince of Tides, *writing about his twin sister Savannah*

[We] started playing together professionally not because we loved the repertory for duo-pianists—we didn't even know it then!—but because we didn't want to separate.

—*Katia Labeque recalling the inspiration for her joint career with her sister Marielle as concert pianists*

Norma Jeane and I sort of perched in the edge of the seat at an angle so we could stare at each other. Every now and then our arms would fly around each other in a hug and we'd look in each other's eyes and say how happy we were. We didn't have anything very original or profound to say. We were both so excited we were almost out of our minds; we were hardly aware of what was going on . . . we sat there like two people who had just fallen in love, I guess. We were overwhelmed at finally getting to see each other; I was so proud of her.

> —*Berniece Baker Miracle recalling her first meeting with her half sister Norma Jeane Baker (later Marilyn Monroe), who was seven years younger and unknown to her until she was 19 and Norma Jeane 12.*

My sister was a true free spirit, independent, full of life. She wore baseball caps before it was popular for women to wear them. She wore sneakers everywhere. And when everyone else in her neighborhood made their babies sunbathe in diapers, she thought it was just fine for her daughter to sleep naked in the sun.

> —*Jean Marks, age 84, mother of two, remembering her sister Fay*

It wouldn't have been like my sister to throw her arms around me the day our mother died, offering extravagant promises of undying approval and devotion. Always an unflinchingly honest person, she offered me the one promise she could wholeheartedly make. "I'm the only one now who remembers the day of your birth," she told me. "No matter what, I will always be your sister."

—Joyce Maynard, novelist and essayist, on her sister Rona

Mauryne was willowy and beautiful in an elusive, turn-of-the-century manner. By the time she was seventeen, she was the most beautiful girl in town, black or white, of which she was keenly aware. She had a small waist and ample hips and long, dark hair that cascaded around her parchment-colored skin. She had the idealized nose of a Greek statue, and her dark eyes were large and round. Her walk was a sensuous, feminine exaggeration of my father's undulating gait. Her persona and good looks were sweetly sexual, like Ava Gardner's. . . .

Walking down the street with Mauryne was an exercise in attraction. Cars honked and stopped, men catcalled, women stared, and teenage girls pointed. She pretended not to notice the havoc she caused on the streets. Stubby and shapeless in my shorts and braids, I was dazzled and proud that this beautiful creature was my big sister.

—Shirlee Taylor Haizlip, writer and producer, recalling her half sister Mauryne

I can remember writing such an enormous quantity of melancholy these last two years in my journal, that it's quite a relief at last to say what fun we have been having. We came home yesterday at half past five in the morning, from Minny's first ball at Mount Felix. I wore a white silk gown and lilac flowers in my hair. Minny had a green wreath and plenty of partners. I had only thirteen. Waltzing is Oh! so delightful and I danced with a cousin of Mr. Synge's who pleased me absurdly by a compliment as to my dancing. Minny looked very nice indeed just as a girl should look. I am so glad that this has been such a good beginning for her.

—Anne Thackeray Ritchie, novelist and daughter of William Thackeray, on her sister Minny's social launch

I hope never to be separated from Anny, except perhaps during my wedding tour. I am sure she will have no reason to regret this change in our lives.

—Minny Thackeray in a letter to a friend about her plans to continue sharing a home with her sister Anne after her marriage

My Childhood's Enchantress

She gave me what no queen could give:
Keys to the secret, How to Live.
Fancy is good, but Faith is better;
I am to my enchantress debtor,
Whose doors swung wide to both. And she—
God sent her hither, long before
I came; he taught sweet mother-lore
To sister-lips. Oh, dear and fair,
My sister with the shining hair.

> —*Lucy Larcom, writer and poet, recalling her beloved sister
> Emmeline in a poem that appeared in the* Boston Transcript,
> *July 27, 1889*

My sister Gigi is the first person I call with good news, so we can celebrate together. Even when I was pregnant and hadn't yet decided whether to tell everyone the sex of my baby, I couldn't resist calling her. No matter what I'm feeling, her response is the one I want to hear before anyone else's. She is my sounding board, my confidante, my keeper of secrets—and my best friend.

> —*Kathleen O'Keefe, mother and business consultant, talking about her
> sister Gigi*

The three of us shared a bedroom, and the bed was our stage. Sug was the Teacher, Beverly was the Mother, and I was the Student, Daisy. Sug would lie flat on the bed and hold me up in the air with her feet on my stomach, and I would pretend to fly and dance, waving my arms around wildly. Bev would watch and offer corrections, "That's not very good," "Straighten your leg." Sug would respond philosophically, "She has talent," or "She didn't do too well in class today." Eventually we became pretty elaborate in our experiments, and my head went through the wall on several occasions.

—Suzanne Farrell, ballerina, writing about her sisters Donna
(known as Sug for Sugar) and Beverly

My Sister;

This is just to greet you this Xmas, to wish you for the next year—knowing you as I do—your heart's desire. . . . Will you take all this in your sweet hands and hug it close against your heart?

. . . Last night, sitting working here, the great jug of scarlet black-berry vine threw a twisted shadow on the wall—rather, my lamp-light, more than a little fascinated, stencilled for me the trailing garlands with a wizard finger, and so I thought of you. Did you get the thought? Did you find it hanging on to the edge of your skirt ("Good gracious, is that a cotton . . . Where *can* I have picked it up" . . .)?

Bless you, my darling, and remember you are always in the heart—oh tucked so close there is no chance of escape—of your sister.

> —*Kathleen Bowden (later Katherine Mansfield) writing to her*
> *younger sister Jeanne Beauchamp, November 10, 1909*

We're just women who admire and really know each other. We allow each other to have the weaknesses the public doesn't allow us to have. . . . We have more energy than any two people on earth. Eventually we run everybody else into the ground.

—*Liza Minelli on her half sister, actress and singer Lorna Luft*

Liza is my best friend and the only person I know I can tell anything to. She never judges me. It's really corny, but she's like a part of me.

—*Lorna Luft, actress and singer, talking about her half sister Liza Minnelli*

When we played store, Fanny was the storekeeper. We used colored glass for money and milkweed puff for rice. When we played school she was the teacher. When we played house she was the mother. But more than that she'd play at reading. Even if she didn't have anything at all to read, she'd imagine it. Before ever going to school, even, she'd pretend. Later she'd climb out the bedroom window to the porch roof where she was all alone and make believe read there.

> —*Sarah Lewis speaking of her sister Fanny, who as Frances Steloff was the founder-owner of the famed Gotham Book Mart (whose motto is "Wise Men Fish Here")*

I had some regrets when my sisters died about not saying "I love you" enough. People don't hug enough and don't say the real *I love yous*.

My sisters knew I loved them, but I was very closemouthed about it. I didn't say it enough, because it was hard for me. But let me tell you, if you have sisters still living, you'd better hug them. You'll regret it if they go and you didn't get a chance to express that feeling. And they'd probably have been waiting for it. I know my sisters were waiting for me.

> —*Patti LaBelle remembering her sisters Jackie, Barbara, and Vivian*

My sister! My little sister—I called her that, in spite of the fact that she was two years older than me. . . . I don't think anyone ever regarded me as a child. . . . Though I am the youngest of three, my brother and sister always looked on me as the oldest. In fact, I can hardly remember ever having felt young, in the ordinary sense. I always had opinions, and the others looked to me for decisions, and for the solutions to their childish problems. But my moods were changeable. Happy one moment, the next plunged in despair. Yet they came to me for help and comfort.

—*Greta Garbo on her sister Alva Gustafson*

Michie and I shared a bedroom—and a deep attachment. Most nights we had this little ritual where we'd stand in the doorway of the room, ready to turn out the lights and hit the sack. Then we had to say, "Jumbug," and jump into bed because there were alligators under the beds, and we'd say, "Good night, good night, good night, you dirty bite." It was gibberish, but we had to do it or we couldn't go to sleep. If one of us was angry, we'd refuse to do it so the other one couldn't fall asleep.

—*Kathie Lee Gifford writing about her younger sister Michele*

[One] thing we have in common is a willingness to accept each other, no matter how difficult it may be. At a sermon that Caroline gave during a recent family reunion, she said, "God puts you in families so you get to know and understand people you otherwise wouldn't." So though our career paths may never cross, I know that we'll be sisters forever, with a lifetime of opportunities to sort things out.

—Lily Burana, stripper and erotica publisher, writing about her sister Caroline, a Presbyterian minister

My sister Shirley is five years younger than I am so I can clearly remember when she was born. I remember her first steps, when she began to talk (very early, and she hasn't shut up since), and the long ordeal of her potty training (she used to scoot around on her shocking pink potty for hours). Because I was more competent at such things as reading and tying my own shoes, I came to consider her my creature.

I remember when I first realized this was no longer so. We must have been fifteen and ten, respectively, when our plane lost a wheel and we were stuck for four days in Damascus. We visited the ruins of Baalbek, and Shirley began instructing me on the "egg-and-dart" frieze. Up to that moment I had never even heard of such things, and I suddenly understood, with a shock, that this child lived an independent life from me and knew about things that I didn't know.

Another turning point in our relationship came when we were twenty-five and twenty. We were having lunch together and I was complaining about a pair of patent leather shoes I'd just bought at Altman's, which had stretched out of shape on the first wearing. Shirley became tremendously indignant and dragged me, protesting, over to Altman's then and there and got my money back. I realized then that I was definitely the more timid of the two.

> —*Gene Young, book editor, talking about her sister Shirley, a General Motors executive*

Lynn and I were both nominated for Oscars that year, I for *Morgan* and she for *Georgy Girl*. I thought Lynny would certainly win the Oscar. She was so comic and so vulnerable, and so totally surprising in every scene she played. However, Elizabeth Taylor had also given an extraordinary performance in *Who's Afraid of Virginia Woolf?* and she got the Academy Award. The press had a whale of a time playing Lynn and me against each other. Actually, I know that if either one of us had won, we would have been pleased. I certainly was really excited and happy to see how my little sister, who had always been treated as an "also-ran" while a child and young teenager, had proved once again my strongest belief—that every child, given half a chance in life, and however unlikely it may seem superficially, has an enormous and totally individual potential to be "a very considerable person." Lynny had truly proved herself before in *Georgy Girl*, in *Mother Courage*, and in *Hay Fever* at the National. In *Georgy Girl* she captured for all people the agony and the comic side of being a lumpy, awkward teenager who can and will become someone very special.

—*Vanessa Redgrave writing about her younger sister Lynn Redgrave*

She took care of me, protected me. When I made the decision to become an actress, she was very supportive. I don't feel I learned about acting from her. Only that it could be done.

—*Lynn Redgrave speaking about her sister, actress Vanessa Redgrave, in an interview*

Hetty seems a good deal more lively than she used to appear at Paris; whether it is that her spirits are better, or that the great liveliness of the inhabitants made her appear grave there by comparison, I know not: but she was there remarkable for being *serieuse*, and is here for being gay and lively. She is a most sweet girl. My sister Fanny is unlike her in almost everything, yet both are very amiable, and love each other as sincerely as ever sisters did. The characteristics of Hetty seem to be wit, generosity, and openness of heart: Fanny's—sense, sensibility, and bashfulness, and even a degree of prudery. Her understanding is superior, but her diffidence gives her a bashfulness before company with whom she is not intimate, which is a disadvantage to her. My eldest sister shines in conversation; . . . were Fanny equally so, I am persuaded she would shine no less. I am afraid that my eldest sister is too communicative, and that my sister Fanny is too reserved. They are both charming girls.

—Englishwoman Susanna Burney at age 14 describing the differences between her older sisters Hetty and Fanny, who was later a renowned 18th-century novelist

I always knew that my parents were proud of their eldest daughter and that, as the second-born girl, I was not really a welcome child. But Simone valorized me even though she could have crushed me by siding with our parents, and that's why I remained attached to her. She was always nice, always defending me against them. In our games when she liked to play the saint, I think it must have given me [unconscious] pleasure to martyrize her even though she was so kind. I remember one day reaching the summit of cruelty: she took the role of a young and beautiful girl whom I, as an evil ruler, was keeping prisoner in a tower. I had the inspiration that my most serious punishment for her would be to tear up her prayer book so she could not pray—a symbolic prayer book, of course, because I would not have dared to harm a real one. But Simone always had the last word in these games. With symbolic glue, she put the prayer book back together. So because of her sainthood, her virtue and especially her determination, she always overcame and she always won.

—*Hélène de Beauvoir speaking about her sister Simone de Beauvoir*

Teaching my sister to read, write, and count gave me, from the age of six onwards, a sense of pride in my own efficiency. I liked scrawling phrases or pictures over sheets of paper: but in doing so I was only creating imitation objects. When I started to change ignorance into knowledge, when I started to impress truths upon a virgin mind, I felt I was at last creating something real. I was not just imitating grown-ups: I was on their level.

—*Simone de Beauvoir describing her closeness to her younger sister Hélène (called Poupette)*

My sisters and I stand, arms around each other, laughing and wiping the tears from each other's eyes. The flash of the Polaroid goes off and my father hands me the snapshot. My sisters and I watch quietly together, eager to see what develops.

The gray-green surface changes to the bright colors of our three images, sharpening and deepening all at once. And although we don't speak, I know we all see it: Together we look like our mother. Her same eyes, her same mouth, open in surprise to see, at last, her long-cherished wish.

—*from* The Joy Luck Club *by Amy Tan*

I talked to my sister Gay this afternoon, you know how wonderfully calm and composed she can be, and how deeply and fearfully she feels everything; and I said, "Oh, it seems so strange to be without him!" And my sister said, "Honey, you know me—I believe we've still got him." Isn't that superb and lovely? And I asked her why she couldn't just take a plane and come up and sit around with me until she got bored—she gets bored pretty easily, more especially with her family, much as she loves us, all of us—and she said, No, "I'll come up next spring, or if I don't, I'll send my ghost—that is all you lack there, no doubt."

—*Katherine Anne Porter writing to a friend about her sister Gay*
Holloway shortly after the death of their brother Paul

When I have Gladys in my arms and press her against my heart I know what love is, at least I know how it feels to love tenderly, truly, deeply, sincerely. My love for her can never change, and when I see how she comes to me in her little troubles or when she is tired and puts two tender arms around my neck and her head on my breast, it makes me feel that here is the pleasure of my life, here is someone who needs and loves to have me.

—*Gertrude Vanderbilt Whitney, arts patron, talking about her little*
sister Gladys

When my twin sisters were born, our mother got sick and was in and out of the hospital much of their lives. So my sisters and I became parents to each other. We were and still are extremely close. They live in Boston and run a clothing business. They work together every day *and* they live within three blocks of each other.

Even though I'm two years older, I never behaved like their mother. I was the flighty, ditzy one when I was growing up. Because our mother was not around, my sisters and I used to do the shopping together, and then we'd come home and clean the entire house every Saturday. My aunt came up from Florida and taught us how to clean. She showed us how to vacuum the venetian blinds and use the dust mop on the floors, how to do the bathroom and toilets. My sisters always gave me the easiest room because I was the slowest one. I'd be in the hallway, cleaning, and they'd say, "Barbara, hurry up, we're all finished."

I'd always act as intermediary for them. When Ilene would worry that Sandy was feeling depressed, she'd ask me to call her. Then Sandy would open up to me in a way she might not to Ilene. I had to be careful, though, not to get caught in the middle. When I was little, I used to take sides sometimes because they were so close and I always felt left out. But every time I did that it would always turn against me. *They* would make up and I'd be left out. But that's how it is with twins. We feel so fortunate that we've been able to come together now and share our lives again. We helped each other grow up, bolstered each other's egos, supported each other through the rough spots, and now it's almost like being kids again, we're so close.

—*Barbara Winkler-Kaplan, Ph.D., fellow in behavioral medicine at Cambridge Hospital (Harvard Medical School), talking about her twin sisters, Ilene and Sandy*

Our father sat us down and told us how we had to always be each other's best friend ... and I know this sounds corny but I can remember the strength in Sharon's eyes. They were so penetrating. It was clear she was taking his always-stick-together instructions very seriously and from that day on, Sharon assumed responsibility for me. We have always been the constant in each other's lives.

—*Bennie Wiley on her closeness to her sister, former Washington, D.C., mayor Sharon Pratt Dixon*

I asked him how I could learn to get along with my sister Mimi. She was twelve then, and very beautiful, and we fought all the time. Not in a big way, but in nasty put-downs and ugly faces, and once in a while nail marks left in each other's arms. It seemed so endless and unkind. Ira said to pretend that it was the last hour of her life, as, he pointed out, it might well be. So I tried out his plan. Mimi reacted strangely at first, as anyone does when a blueprint is switched on him without his being consulted. I learned to look at her, and as a result, to see her for the first time. I began to love her. The whole process took about one summer. It's curious, but there is perhaps no one in the world as dear to me as Mimi.

—*Joan Baez (at age 16) talking about her sister Mimi*

Belinda turned away to meet Harriet, who was moving towards her through the crowd. Her face radiated joy and happiness. How nice it is that Harriet is entering so whole-heartedly into their feelings, thought Belinda, for she had been so afraid that her sister might be made unhappy by the curate's marriage and departure.

"The third from the left," whispered Harriet eagerly.

Belinda looked about her, rather puzzled. Then she saw what her sister meant, for in a corner she saw five curates, all young and pale and thin, with the exception of one, who was tall and muscular and a former Rugby Blue, as she afterwards learned.

The third from the left. How convenient of the curates to arrange themselves so that Belinda could so easily pick out Harriet's choice. He was dark and rather Italian-looking, paler and more hollow-cheeked than the others. Now Belinda understood her sister's joy and suddenly she realized that she too was happier than she had been for a long time.

—*from* Some Tame Gazelle *by Barbara Pym*

Monday July 4th.

Dearest Arabel's birthday. She is 18; and an interesting intelligent amiable feeling girl. I should love her even if she were not my sister; & even if she did not love me.

—*Elizabeth Barrett (Browning) writing in her diary about her sister Arabella on July 4, 1831*

I knew every inch of the ground and precincts before we were first taken there [the Tower of London], walked without hesitation to stand by Traitor's Gate, and then pointed out, correctly, the name of every tower commanding the walls. Had I not beheaded Jeanne, time and time again, on Tower Green? I knew the identical spot where the block had stood. "How nobly she walks to her death," I heard one of the maids whisper, when Tower Green had been the garden of the moment. Jeanne, strutting past, certainly made a moving figure, her curls pinned on the top of her head, while I, the axeman, waited, walking stick in hand—the crook of the handle forming the axe—and, as was the rightful custom, dropped on one knee to ask her pardon before I felled her with a single blow.

Angela always took the women's parts. She was splendid as Bloody Mary, for whom she vowed she had a real affection, but the trouble with Angela, as the years passed, was that she soon lost interest, once a game had started, and would suddenly say, "Oh, I don't think I want to play after all," and wander off on some ploy of her own . . . Jeanne showed more enthusiasm and, being nearly four years my junior, proved malleable to my direction, switching from role to role, one moment Gog the giant and the next Xit the dwarf, but more often the hapless victim of the executioner's axe. I have no recollection of ever suffering that hideous fate myself, though on occasion I would stretch myself upon the rack, or better still writhe, attacked by rodents, in the notorious Rat Pit.

—*Daphne du Maurier reminiscing about playing with her sisters Angela and Jeanne*

Not long after our family moved from the hectic street life of Queens, New York, to a very quiet, very proper Westchester suburb, my mother acquired a Super-8 movie camera. My sister was twelve and I was eleven, and we decided that we would create a cooking show, in the tradition of Julia Child and the Galloping Gourmet. Their shows were full of the sparkling Caucasian perfection that we longed for.

We planned our show with zeal and piety. It would be a live broadcast, to give it more urgency. I would be the host, and my sister the cameraman and director. The day's recipe would be shortbread cookies, made using a shiny aluminum "cookie gun"— another of my mother's newly acquired suburban devices. Everything was laid out with a great deal of fussing and bickering: with my sister and me, there is much crudeness, unveiled crankiness, and psychic shorthand. This makes for good creative teamwork.

I have on my flowered apron. The butter and flour are measured and ready. My sister turns on the old-fashioned, blindingly bright camera spotlight, and cries, "Action!" At first, everything is fine. I speak with the smooth warmth I associate with cooking show hosts; I mix and roll with ease. Then, I stumble over a word and my chirpy facade falters. I spot my sister's expression, and at that moment we both know, wordlessly, that we want this to be a different kind of cooking show. My monologue becomes more and more off-center; the cookie gun malfunctions and I have to bang it on the counter; the cookies turn out burned. Every time I do something strange, my sister smiles wildly, encouragingly. By the end, the host, thinking the camera is off, is weeping, bemoaning the loss of ratings and sponsors. She absentmindedly munches on a cookie, and shudders at its taste. As she throws up into a mixing bowl, she looks up to find that she is still on live television. And that is how our show ends.

—Mari Hatta, filmmaker, on her earliest collaboration with her sister Kayo, years before their award-winning film Picture Bride

Myrna's visits were like royalty coming to town. She wore African clothes and looked regal. A talented painter and photographer, she sometimes used me as a subject. I always sat very still and she'd say I was a perfect model. It made me proud to be the perfect anything.

Myrna's voice was like a flowing river, calm and filled with musical inflections. In my mother's house, even when we were calm, we'd be screaming and yelling, talking at the same time. Myrna would always wait until things had almost calmed down to add her comments.

Myrna called me Bess-One, her number one. She'd tell me African folk tales and would let me help her paint. I used to think that our backyard on Gordon Street was full of trees, but there was only one tree. All the others I remember came from Myrna's paintings.

>—*Bertice Berry, Ph.D., describing her eldest sister Myrna, who started all her letters with: "Dear Bessie, my beloved, most beautiful sister."*

Natalie was my surrogate parent, the person I knew would protect me from any danger. One night Mother got us up in matching red dresses, and she and Pop took us out to dinner. We were driving across a bridge when Natalie saw a car strike a child. Natalie gasped in horror, and when I looked up to see what was happening, Natalie pulled me into her lap and hid my face in her arms. I struggled a bit as my curiosity got the best of me, but Natalie's embrace was as complete as it was tense, and I remained in her arms, my face buried on her chest. She held me hard, her body rigid. I knew I was safe.

—*Lana Wood writing about her sister, actress Natalie Wood*

Dear—

Am sending you twenty dollars. If you can't make that do all right, telegraph me—or, no, Hunk, I'll just send you twenty-five instead, & let you save all you can of it. It's going to be hard, baby,—we'll probably want money pretty bad pretty often,—but no unworthy girl ever had so many friends as I have, & we shan't starve, because we *can* borrow.—I'm as crazy to see you as if I were going to be married to you—no one is such good pals as we are . . .

—*Edna St. Vincent Millay inviting her younger sister Norma to join her in Greenwich Village*

My sister, who would have been sixteen or seventeen at the time, was strong willed and persuasive. My mother must, that summer, have been under her spell, for she let Olga drill me for hours every day on the beach, in preparation for taking a ballet exam. This exam was of no concern to me (except as Olga urged me toward it) and indeed I had no idea of what it would be like to take any exam, since I didn't go to school but "did lessons" at home. And whether or not I became particularly proficient in dancing was certainly not of concern to our mother. However, it was for the moment Olga's obsession; and so each day she put me through my paces—"*barre*," for which some wall or stair-railing was used in lieu of an actual bar; "floorwork"—*attitudes* and *arabesques* and *port de bras*; and "elevation" (which was what I liked best, the *jetés* and *grand jetés* and other leaps and bounds).

. . . Olga, with all her phenomenal energy and dedication, shouted and counted and made up *enchainements* and urged me beyond my natural capacities and inclinations. I would get cross or even tearful at times; but though I had my moments of being *fed-up*, I didn't really hate all this. Olga could scold fiercely but she always flattered as well, so that my self-esteem was reinforced; and I really did love the sense of having graceful arms and strong "elevation."

—*Denise Levertov, poet, writing about her older sister Olga*

My sister and I perform a show called "Sibling Revelry." Every time we walk on stage, I see not only a beautiful woman who's going to blow the roof off with her great voice, but I also see the little baby I met when I was nearly three who was crying so loud we should have known she was destined for Broadway. I see the awkward girl wanting to fit in, the girl too shy to perform in front of anyone, the girl who announced "if all else fails I guess I could always sing." And I see the person with whom I learned year after year about life and love and divorce and death and marriage and birth and dreams.

And so when we begin to sing, I feel an unspeakable joy in knowing that we are living our dreams and we are celebrating our survival. For there, as we carefully blend our two voices into one, are all the stories of our lives that we have shared through the years. And there, on the sixty-fifth floor of Rockefeller Center or on the stage of Carnegie Hall, I am doing what I love and do best with the person who knows me best.

It is in these moments I revel in the truth that sisterhood *is* powerful.

—Ann Hampton Callaway, singer-songwriter, writing about her sister, Broadway actress and singer Liz Callaway

Ann and I were definitely *not* best friends when we were growing up. You know, the typical sibling rivalry . . . But I remember the night before she left for college: I was in a miserable mood and picked a big fight with her. She yelled, "What's wrong with you?" I just broke down and cried that I was going to miss her. I guess I hadn't realized until that moment how much I loved her. A few months later I went to visit her at school. We got drunk together, and I do believe we have been the best of friends ever since!

(Three years later, we moved to New York City together, and now, sixteen years later, we have the great fun and privilege of doing our show, called "Sibling Revelry," together!)

—Liz Callaway, Broadway actress and singer, talking about her sister, singer-songwriter Ann Hampton Callaway

I had always thought that when we grew old it would be Ea who would gather us all together, and it would be at her home that we would talk about the old memories; it was probably because she was the only one of us to have a child that I thought that she and her home would be the center for our generation, but above all because she was so radiant, glowingly loving and sharing. But now I feel that in a way, now she is gone, she is binding us even more closely together. I do not know whether Ea was as kind to anyone else as she was to me. I think constantly of those last days when I was at home . . . I seem still to feel her warm loving arms around me.

> —*Isak Dinesen, author of* Out of Africa, *writing to her sister Ellen Dahl just after the death of their sister Inger (Ea)*

Daphne made friends at that school though she could never ask them home to our dungeon. We did have these social unaccepta-bilities: a crippled father, a teacher mother and lived in substandard habitations. But Daphne sailed right over this. For a start, who could resist the shining golden-brown curls to her shoulders, the sparkling touching green eyes, her pretty hands and legs. Above all she made people laugh, even her teachers. She didn't even have to try. At times she didn't even say anything; she'd just look at you, that's all, and you'd find yourself beginning to tremble with laughter. People pay anything, put up with anything for this.

> —*Sylvia Ashton-Warner, author and educator, recalling her sister Daphne's charms*

Look out of the window, & see what a fine prospect. The Clinton river winds gently & slowly along in the valley, just below the window. This beautiful stream with its green banks, and picturesk islands, is enough to compensate one for the want of many other conveniences. When I am sad or lonely I sit here & gaze out upon the beautiful scene, till my heart grows better and happyer. They are sometimes cheering moments & how I do wish my dear sister Lucy was here, to share every thought & feeling. I think of you then Lucy, & I think of *home* while a thousand strange thoughts, plans, anticipations, & emotions crowd around till my heart aches & my brain becomes almost giddy. But the low murmuring of that river has power to sooth again till every thought is tranquil as its own pure water.

—Antoinette Louisa Brown Blackwell in an 1846 letter to her
beloved sister-in-law, women's rights advocate Lucy Stone

Babe, Betsey, and Minnie were known throughout Manhattan—and even beyond—as "the Fabulous Cushing Sisters." Babe by then was in her early twenties, Betsey in her late twenties, and Minnie in her early thirties. Betsey was the most ladylike and sensitive-looking. She had blue eyes and a fair complexion; her delicate features were pretty, but not as dramatic as Babe's. Minnie had fine, thin features as well, but was the least attractive. . . .

With their dark, wavy hair parted identically on the left and falling just below the neck, the Cushing girls were seen everywhere together. "The three of them had enormous sense," recalled Diana Vreeland. "They had the sort of minds that were curious about beautiful things. They had a basic sense of taste, a basic look about the bones in their faces. They were built like Americans. There was a moment when they were extraordinary."

> *—Sally Bedell Smith describing the glamorous Babe (married to William Paley), Betsey (married first to a Roosevelt, then to Jock Whitney) and Minnie (who was mistress, then wife, to Vincent Astor)*

Brenda was born after I got married. I told her to change her professional name to Crystal Gayle when she started her own singing career because we didn't want her to get confused with Brenda Lee. I didn't know Brenda too closely when she was growing up, but Peggy Sue was my first sister, and I claimed her right away. When she was born, I ran up and down Butcher Holler, shouting, "I got a baby sister, I got the prettiest baby sister in the whole world!"

—Loretta Lynn on two of her sisters, Peggy Sue (who wrote several hit songs with her sister), and Brenda, later Crystal Gayle, who followed her older sister into a country music career

My only sister, five years older than I, died when she was forty. She was over six feet tall, too, by an angstrom unit or so. She was heavenly to look at, and graceful, both in and out of the water. She was a sculptress. She was christened "Alice," but she used to deny that she was really an Alice. I agreed. Everybody agreed. Sometime in a dream maybe I will find out what her real name was.

—Kurt Vonnegut remembering his sister Alice

To Anna

Sister, dear, when you are lonely,
　　Longing for your distant home,
And the images of loved ones
　　Warmly to your heart shall come,
Then, mid tender thoughts and fancies
　　Let one fond voice say to thee,
"Ever when your heart is heavy,
　　Anna, dear, then think of me."
Think how we two have together
　　Journeyed onward day by day,
Joys and sorrows ever sharing,
　　While the swift years roll away.
Then may all the sunny hours
　　Of our youth rise up to thee,
And when your heart is light and happy,
　　Anna, dear, then think of me.

—Poem by 12-year-old Louisa May Alcott written for her sister
Anna during a time when they were separated

We got into show business when we were very young. In 1932, we were already singing. LaVerne was about seventeen, Patty was twelve, I was fourteen. Three Minneapolis girls with a Greek father and a Norwegian mother. We all loved the Boswell Sisters. The Boswells had broken the barrier between semiclassical and New Orleans jazz for white singers. We imitated them—even their accents. We must have sounded pretty good, because we got signed up by a big unit show. Unit Shows—one orchestra and a lot of acts—were the dying gasp of vaudeville. That show closed just about every beautiful R.K.O. theatre in the Middle West. But the managers took a rich sense of responsibility for my sisters and me. They taught us the discipline of the theatre: you showed up half an hour before the curtain went up, and you never peeked through it.

LaVerne had a wonderful music memory. She figured things out. She would listen to a Boswell Sisters record and then teach me and Patty the parts. She loved swing music, too. Once—I forget where, maybe in Cleveland—we heard a band playing and they had three trumpets, in harmony, and she said, "There, kids, we have to learn to sing like those trumpets."

> —*Maxene Andrews recalling how she and her sisters LaVerne and Patty started out as the Andrews Sisters*

Willa liked to tell a story of three-year-old Elsie. One season had been dry and everyone was hoping for rain. When Elsie asked her mother what made the rain, her mother said that God did. The next day for the first time that season, a neighbor in desperation turned on his two lawn sprinklers. Elsie came running in calling for "Willie" and explaining that there were *two* little gods out in the neighbor's yard, just raining like everything.

> —*Willa Cather reminiscing about her sister Elsie as recalled in* The World of Willa Cather

> Lord help the mister
> Who comes between me and my sister,
> And lord help the sister
> Who comes between me and my man!

> —*from "Sisters" by Irving Berlin, sung by Rosemary Clooney and Vera-Ellen in* White Christmas

I remember coming to visit her once, and she had a suite at the Chateau Marmont—a great, glamorous suite. And I said, "Oh, this is lovely, great!" She snapped, "Yes, you won't actually be sleeping here. There is a little room at the top of the hotel where you will be sleeping." I found at night Warren [Beatty] would change places with me. He would sleep in the suite, and I would be in his little attic room. . . .

I got propositioned by Warren. But since I turned his proposition down, we've never shared a boyfriend.

> —*Jackie Collins describing early days in Hollywood with her sister Joan Collins*

Once in a while Ann and I write letters. "My begonias are blooming," she said in one, "and I don't even *like* them." Only between ourselves and a very few others dare we expose such examples of ugly ingratitude. When we meet, twice a year or so, we discover odd similarities. We both smile at ourselves in the mirror and say "Hi!" even if nobody is looking. When we wake under the same roof and meet in the kitchen for breakfast, we stride manfully toward each other, parodying *macho* salesmen at a conference, with hearty jock handshakes and deep-voiced self-introductions:
"Ann Condon."
"Jane Howard."

> —*Jane Howard, journalist and biographer, writing about her sister Ann*

My little sister was different. Being perfect was of no interest whatsoever to her. She was a tomboy, she got into scrapes, she hardly ever did what she was told—in short, she never tried to fit anybody else's idea of what her "role" should be. I was the sweet one, and Andrea was the rowdy one. At least, "sweet" was the word all my relatives used. "Loni is so sweet," they'd say approvingly. "But that Andrea, she's something else again."

And she was a handful. Mom used to joke, "We would've had more children, but for Andrea. And if she had been the first, she would have been the only." My dad called her Ornerya; draw a line in the dirt, stand back, and count the seconds before Andrea would go over it.

She literally *did* cross a line once. She crawled out into the middle of the street when she was about eighteen months old. I wasn't quite five, and I stood there like a dutiful statue and watched her do it. Because we had been told: Stay in the yard. Andrea had all her little cars lined up, pushing them up and down the white line. And I couldn't move. Finally I ran inside in a panic and told my mother the baby was out in the street. Mom was appropriately horror-struck and snatched her up in a heartbeat. I couldn't understand why *I* was scolded.

—*Loni Anderson writing about her sister Andrea*

My sister Emily loved the moors. Flowers brighter than the rose bloomed in the blackest of the heath for her; out of a sullen hollow in a livid hill-side her mind could make an Eden. She found in the bleak solitude many and dear delights; and not the least and best loved was—liberty.

—*Charlotte Brontë on her sister Emily*

"If Cassandra were going to have her head cut off, Jane would insist on sharing her fate."

—*quote attributed to Cassandra Austen, mother of Jane Austen and her sister Cassandra, circa 1780s*

I had made several attempts to snuff baby Amy in her cradle. Mother had repeatedly discovered me pouring glasses of water carefully into her face. So when Molly had appeared, Mother had led me to believe the new baby was a kind of present for me. Actually, the baby displaced Amy. I liked everything about her—the strong purity of her cheeriness, bewilderment, outrage; her big dumb baldness, pointy fingers, little teeth, the works.

Molly possessed a dingy blanket, which she trailed behind her like a travois on her crawls. During this period, she held the belief that when she herself could not see, she was invisible. Consequently, in order to hide, she draped her head in this blanket. When it was time for her nap, we found her a pyramidal woolly mound on the pantry floor, a veritable monadnock, her fat foot protruding from the blanket's edge. She barely breathed from suspense. It broke her heart to be discovered and bundled away, day after day; she tried hard to hide, ever more motionless.

When the spirit of Lister seized Mother, she flung the appalling blanket into the washing machine. Molly wept inconsolably, so Mother carried her to the basement to let her watch the thing go around in the dryer. Molly plumped down intently, straight-backed, before the dryer as if it were a television screen; her big head rolled around and around on her tiny neck. Mother, Amy, and I watched from the top of the stairs, trying not to let her hear us. Finally, Mother cut the blanket in two so she could wash one easily, and that particular joke was over.

—*Annie Dillard, writer, on her sisters Amy and Molly*

My sister is never still. Even as a child she was filled with a restless energy that swung her around flagpoles and into water fountains with parents and grandparents scrambling in her wake. My sister sings in bursts, like gunfire, and she swings her arms as if rowing through air. She doesn't like fresh fruit except for pears shaped like pregnant women, and crunchy. She eats them when she's driving, tearing the skin with her teeth. Her hair is cut short with twirls over her ears like an opera singer's and her eyebrows are black and straight, no need for eyebrow pencils. When she was sixteen a fortune teller told her she would find success in a faraway country, and marry twice. When she left us she changed the way she walked and dressed and talked, and also her name. For years I stubbornly used her old name. . . . Once I could never have imagined going anywhere without her, but nowadays we see each other only every two or three years, for two or three weeks. We live in cities at opposite ends of the world, where we can pretend we are completely unique.

—*Beth Yahp, Australian writer, on her sister*

I lived in a little cocoon of family. I was never lonely. As soon as I could walk and talk I lived an intensely imaginative life. On Sunday afternoons my father would take me for a walk. This was a special event. We went right down to the little brook and played "pooh sticks" and on the way home I visited all my "friends." Certain bushes and trees along the country lanes housed fairies, and we used to knock at a bush, enter, and have tea and a chat. . . .

When I was three and a half my mother presented me with a sister, Lindsey Madeleine. She was too young to play with for a long time. She was a noisy, vivacious baby and extremely restless. As soon as she could sit up, she ruined the pram by forcing her head through the canvas hood. We must have looked an odd trio on our afternoon walks, my mother pushing a battered and muddy pram with Lindsey's head thrust through the hole in the hood, like the figurehead on the prow of a ship, waiting patiently while I stood chattering into a thornbush.

—*Karen Armstrong, writer and teacher, remembering her baby sister Lindsey*

Going out with Brigitte one night, she whispered to me, "Watch out, there are photographers just over there." I was so angry at the way they kept stalking her, at the way they were so obsessed with her and at the way they were ruining her life, that I took off my shoe and threatened them with it. I screamed at the top of my voice, "Leave us alone. Go away." Brigitte thought it was hilarious and the next morning there was the photo in the papers, of a crazy younger sister waving her shoe and, behind her, Brigitte with an angelic smile.

> —*Mijanou Bardot talking about her sister, film legend Brigitte Bardot*

Only Elizabeth was an artist to her fingertips, and whichever of her talents she used, she used it differently from all the rest of us. Her perceptions, so different from ours, have nourished me throughout the years. Her understanding of what has gone on in schools has provided depth and life to my own observations on American education. And her paintings have made every place I have lived in my home.

> —*Margaret Mead on her sister Elizabeth*

From the time we were little girls I always felt like I was Robin's protector. I can remember when we were small, Robin didn't like milk. But she would drink it if I tasted it for her first. We've just always had this understanding that I would always look out for her.

—*Stephanie Givens speaking of her sister, actress Robin Givens*

"Ursula," said Gudrun, "don't you really *want* to get married?" Ursula laid her embroidery in her lap and looked up. Her face was calm and considerate.

"I don't know, " she replied. "It depends how you mean."

Gudrun was slightly taken aback. She watched her sister for some moments.

"Well," she said ironically, "it usually means one thing!—But don't you think anyhow, you'd be"—she darkened slightly—"in a better position than you are in now?"

A shadow came over Ursula's face.

"I might," she said. "But I'm not sure."

Again Gudrun paused, slightly irritated. She wanted to be quite definite.

"You don't think one needs the *experience* of having been married?" she asked.

"Do you think it need *be* an experience?" replied Ursula.

"Bound to be, in some way or other," said Gudrun, coolly. "Possibly undesirable, but bound to be an experience of some sort."

"Not really," said Ursula. "More likely to be the end of experience."

—*from* Women in Love *by D. H. Lawrence*

Strictly speaking, before I broke my nose, I was better-looking than Laura, but she had rarer and more beautiful eyes. Brains are such a small part of people that I cannot judge of them between her and me; and, at the age of twenty-three, when she died, few of us are at the height of our powers; but Laura made and left a deeper impression on the world in her short life than anyone I have ever known. What she really had to a greater degree than other people was true spirituality, a feeling of intimacy with the other world and a sense of the love and wisdom of God and His plan of life. This did not prevent her from being a very great flirt. The first time that a man came to Glen and liked me better than Laura, she was immensely surprised—not more so than I was—and had it not been for the passionate love which we cherished for each other, there must inevitably have been much jealousy between us.

> —*Margot Asquith, Victorian writer and Prime Minister's wife, recalling her closeness to her sister Laura Tennant*

June looked as though she belonged in the theatre. Her eyes were large and very blue, with deep circles under them. Even before Mother touched June's hair up with peroxide, it was bright yellow. Her legs were long and wiry, with bumpy knees. Mother massaged the bumps every night with cold cream, but they never went away. Even if this had been serious it wouldn't have mattered, because Mother's mind was made up. Her daughters were going to have a theatrical career.

We made our debut, with Grandpa's halfhearted permission, and his money for costumes, at one of his lodges. It was a Knights of Pythias celebration following the installation of officers, and Grandpa played piano for us. He played for the installation of officers, too; it was because of his connection with the lodge that Mother managed to book our act.

I sang "I'm a Hard-Boiled Rose" in a "tough" costume—a sweater and skirt, a feathered hat, and striped stockings—but the evening belonged to my sister. From the moment she stepped on the stage in her pink tarlatan ballet dress, with a butterfly in her hair, the audience was hers.

—Gypsy Rose Lee writing about her sister, actress June Havoc

I always describe my younger sister, Tanya, as the antithesis of me. She possesses the body of a Hollywood pin-up while I possess that of a carpenter's dream. She always has a contagious smile on her lovely face and I a serious "don't-mess-with-me" look. Tanya does things to please herself while I, the dutiful daughter, constantly strive to meet my parents' expectations. In essence, my sister Tanya lives life to the fullest, smelling the roses along the way, while I toil away for tomorrow, never really experiencing today.

For just once in my life I would love to run freely on the beach, binge on all 31 flavors of Baskin-Robbins ice cream, let the dishes pile up in the sink, play hooky from work for a day, and drive for miles with no particular destination or arrival time. Perhaps then I might be able to experience a whole new side of life that has eluded me for years but brought fulfillment and freedom to Tanya. But then who would be there to watch out for my parents and lift my sister up when she occasionally stumbles? There I go, worrying about tomorrow. . . .

—*Tamara Nikuradse, marketing manager and author of* My Mother Had a Dream, *on her sister Tanya, an aspiring flight attendant*

My sisters were musically abused. That is the only way I can think of to describe what I put them through in my constant search for musical satisfaction. Stella and Cassie were my chief victims. Of course, I was always the star, and I made them sing backup. I would use any kind of promise, threat, or coercion to get them to do what I wanted. "Oh, I'll do your chores if you'll just sing one more verse," or "I'll tell Mama about your boyfriend if you don't sing one more verse," or "I'll just die and it will be your fault if you don't sing one more verse."

There was one period of time when I just knew I had hit upon a surefire formula for instant stardom. I would have my reluctant backup sisters sing in pig Latin. Brenda Lee had not thought of this; what a silly oversight on her part. This was going to be the biggest thing that ever hit radio, TV, or the special live stage that would surely be built so that the entire world could hear us sing, "E-shay, as-way I-may est-bay end-fray." (Translation: She was my best friend.) I had made up all of the parts, and I wanted to hear them. It was of no consequence to me whether my sisters wanted to sing them. It simply had to be done. Even today, if I start into one of our old arrangements, Stella and Cassie will chime in with their parts. I had them so drilled. Somehow pig-Latin backup singing never caused quite the stir I expected it to; we never even made it onto "the Ed Sullivan Show." Stella and Cassie are probably just as glad that it didn't.

—Dolly Parton on singing with her sisters Stella and Cassie

To Bee, my old chum. . . .

I have formed quite a romantic affection for my dear little sister of fourteen and describe her eyes, music, and all in the most glowing terms. Only I beseech you not to turn my present happiness into green-eyed jealousy by taking a mean advantage of my absence and becoming most awfully and scornfully learned, and looking down upon me as quite beneath your notice. If you do, I shall certainly come back to the schoolroom again—which perhaps won't suit you, my dear!

> —*Maggie Potter writing to her sister Beatrice, future social reformer and cofounder with husband Sidney Webb of the London School of Economics*

For as long as I can remember, Anne wanted to be a novelist. Her head was filled with stories to tell. She came home and wrote, and it got her through every experience. She's as thorough a writer in her heart and soul as anyone I've ever met.

> —*Tamara O'Brien on her sister Anne Rice*

I thought I heard the baby cry, but when I ran to the living room I knew she was not crying nor had she been burned and gone up the chimney. She had turned over and was crawling toward the Christmas tree. Her little-fingered hands were on the floor, her nightgown was hiked over her diapers. I had never seen Bonny crawl before and I watched her with the first feelings of love and pride, the old hostility gone forever.

I played with Bonny with a heart cleansed of jealousy and joyful for the first time in many months. I was reconciled that Santa Claus was only family, but with this new tranquility I felt maybe my family and Jesus Christ were somehow kin. Soon afterward, when we moved to a new house in the suburbs, I taught Bonny how to walk and even let her hold the monkey while I played the organ grinder.

—from "The Discovery of Christmas" by Carson McCullers

I think now of a time when she wanted me to straighten out her library. This was many years ago but even at that period it was difficult for her to walk with a cane for more than a few steps and she wanted to be able to tell whoever happened to be taking care of her at the time exactly where to put his hands on the Rilke poems, *Out of Africa*, *A Portrait of the Artist as a Young Man*, and on and on; it soon became clear that all the books she had were essential to her. Two young girls had come to help with the physical labor of making our homemade version of a library. It was obvious that the girls had not read much and had never read Carson McCullers or heard of her. They just knew that she was a writer and one asked if she had really read all those books. I was busy trying to narrow down the absolutely essential books so that they would fit in one bookcase when I heard the same girl making more polite conversation by saying, "I never did understand why that lady let Beth die in *Little Women*." I didn't want to look at Sister, but the reflex was too sudden and now, thank God, I often see her expression of that moment when I think of her, rather than the way she was those last weeks. Her smile was so sweet and bemused, and she answered gently, seriously, "Yes, I cried too."

—*Margarita G. Smith remembering her sister, writer Carson McCullers*

Elinor had a blithe way of skipping what might seem intolerable difficulties to other people. Once when I felt the noose of marriage growing very tight around my silly throat, and showed twenty-year-old despair about it, she took one look at my terrified face—I was cowering in the bathroom, which I considered the only sanctuary left in the house where I could hide, for the other rooms seemed piled, to me, with wedding presents, a veil, a dress of white satin, boxes of cake and congratulatory letters—and she rescued me with an understanding smile. She said, "Why get married if you don't want to?"

. . . At the time it was a miracle of comprehension for which I was deeply grateful. Her prophecies came true. I was much happier, not obliged to get married, and the young man in question has admitted since that he also was much happier. We have become fast friends. Elinor did not seem angry, whereas everyone else, except my younger brother, looked on me for a few days with mingled curiosity and horror. She said blithely that the proposed wedding had given her a good excuse to buy a new dress and that I was, please, to keep the earrings she had given me.

—*Nancy Hoyt on her sister, Elinor Wylie, poet and novelist*

"Why *don't* we yell at each other?" says Four.

"Because," says One, we're so in love with the idea of our family continuing that to speak truly and honestly would jeopardise it."

"Isn't that a bit pathetic, though? I think we should yell at each other."

"You start."

"All right. 'Get out of my sight, you moll.' How's that?"

"This is *serious*, Four—do you mind?"

"OK. Sorry. But you did yell at me once—don't you remember? I came over to borrow some money and you lost your temper."

"I remember now. I yelled at you that you were so selfish you never asked me how I was, or anything about *my* life—all you did was whine about *your* problems. You bawled and howled, it was dreadful, and I said, 'I'm sorry if this hurts you,' and you said, howling away, 'It's all right, because I need to know why nobody likes me.' And that of course was so tragic that *I* started bawling, and then you looked at me with your red eyes and said in a weird, polite, choked sort of voice, 'And how's work going lately?' We both cracked up laughing—and then I lent you $500 and you went home."

> *—Helen Garner writing about two of her sisters whom she declines to name, instead giving them the numbers of their birth order*

When we were small children, we always huddled in a circle by the door to pray together before my mother left for work. Each person had his or her day to pray. For my sister Debora, it was her first prayer. She began, "Dr. God, bless us all during our day, open our minds so that we can learn, help Mama catch the bus on time, and help all of the people rise from the dead." We still laugh about this.

—*Denyce Graves, opera singer, on her sister Debora*

My Sister, My Friend

When I was looking average, she'd always comb my hair;
She'd manicure my fingernails and show me what to wear.
As a friend I saw her showing me a different kind of fun,
As a sister I learned that *average* was meant for *anyone*.

When I was feeling lonely, across the miles she'd phone;
She'd often send me flowers and sometimes fly me home.
As a friend I felt her hugs and words to make me laugh,
As a sister I felt her guide my feet to put me back on the right
  path.

She taught me about diplomacy, self-respect, and pride.
How to rise to the occasion, never let things slide;
She always exemplified culture, dignity and class.
Showed me how to build my strength, drawing on the past.

To this day, she continues to encourage me, and whenever I am
  down,
She faces the problem with me and drives it into the ground.
So with this poem I honor her, and forever will contend,
There is no friend like my sister, and there's no sister like my
  friend.

   —*Debora Martin, temp agency owner, on her sister, opera singer Denyce*
   Graves

When we were thirteen our parents got us twin beds. Know what we did? We put a violin case in her bed, covered it up, and the two of us slept in mine. By fifteen, it got doggone crowded in there.

—*Abigail Van Buren (Dear Abby), known as Popo, talking about her sister Ann Landers, known as Eppie*

"You are my own flesh, and I love you tenderly; in my heart I love you. I could prove it now by giving you the only thing that has ever been mine: then you would have it all. Please, Verena," she said, faltering, "let this one thing belong to me."

—*Dolly Talbo pleading with her sister Verena in Truman Capote's* The Grass Harp *to let her keep secret the recipe for her herbal medicine*

"Really, girls, you are both to be blamed," said Meg, beginning to lecture in her elder sisterly fashion. "You are old enough to leave off boyish tricks and behave better, Josephine. It didn't matter so much when you were a little girl; but now you are so tall, and turn up your hair, you should remember that you are a young lady."

"I ain't! And if turning up my hair makes me one, I'll wear it in two tails till I'm twenty," cried Jo, pulling off her net and shaking down a chestnut mane. "I hate to think I've got to grow up and be Miss March, and wear long gowns, and look as prim as a China aster. It's bad enough to be a girl, anyway, when I like boys' games, and work, and manners. I can't get over my disappointment in not being a boy, and it's worse than ever now, for I'm dying to go and fight with papa, and I can only stay at home and knit like a poky old woman;" and Jo shook the blue army sock till the needles rattled like castanets, and her ball bounded across the room.

"Poor Jo; it's too bad! But it can't be helped, so you must try to be contented with making your name boyish, and playing brother to us girls," said Beth, stroking the rough head at her knee with a hand that all the dish-washing and dusting in the world could not make ungentle in its touch.

"As for you, Amy," continued Meg, "you are altogether too particular and prim. Your airs are funny now, but you'll grow up an affected little goose if you don't take care. I like your nice manners, and refined ways of speaking, when you don't try to be elegant; but your absurd words are as bad as Jo's slang."

"If Jo is a tomboy and Amy a goose, what am I, please?" asked Beth, ready to share the lecture.

"You're a dear, and nothing else," answered Meg warmly; and no one contradicted her, for the "Mouse" was the pet of the family.

—*from* Little Women *by Louisa May Alcott*

Dear Sister,

I was very glad to hear from you, though there was something in your letters very monstrous and shocking. I wonder with what conscience you can talk to me of your being an old woman; I beg I may hear no more on't. For my part, I pretend to be as young as ever, and really am as young as needs to be, to all intents and purposes. I attribute all this to your living so long at Chatton, and fancy a week at Paris will correct such wild imaginations, and set things in a better light. My cure for lowness in spirits is not drinking nasty water, but galloping all day, and a moderate glass of champagne at night in good company; and I believe this regimen, closely followed, is one of the most wholesome that can be described, and may save one a world of filthy doses, and more filthy doctor's fees at year's end. . . .

Doctor Swift and Johnny Gay are at Pope's, and their conjunction has produced a ballad, which, if nobody else has sent you, I will, being never better pleased than when I am endeavoring to amuse my dear sister. . . .

> —*Lady Mary Wortley Montagu writing to her sister, the Countess of Mar*

My sister, I should say, is an absolute knock-out beauty. I don't know where she gets it from. My mother is quite pretty, but in a twittering, soft sort of way, and so am I, I suppose, whereas Louise has a real old aristocratic predatory grandeur. As tags go, she is *grande dame* while I am *jeune fille*, and she leads all her life to match it. She has a very pale skin and fabulous eyebrows and black hair and a tall, stiletto sort of figure and so forth. I thought to myself, as the train went past all the back views of houses that mean Calais, that perhaps Stephen was marrying her because she never looked ridiculous. At worse he could call her aquiline and intense, but even that sounds quite impressive. Perhaps he wanted a wife to be a figurehead to his triumphal car, a public admiring ornament to his house. A hostess. But I couldn't see what there was in that for her; she was never a great one for playing second fiddle. On the contrary, she was inclined to be ruthless about getting what she wanted. I supposed it was possible that she wanted Stephen.

—Sarah reflecting on her sister Louise's forthcoming marriage in Margaret Drabble's A Summer Bird-Cage

All three of my sisters, who had many other virtues as well, got the Beauty flashcard. JoAnn and Melody were both about five-foot-ten and stunning; Melody was endowed with a spectacular body that drove guys crazy. (With her body and my personality, for sure I'd have ended up in adult films by the time I was sixteen.) While they were dark brunettes, Christal was a blond, blue-eyed, fair-skinned angel, the Miss Congeniality of our family.

The Beauty flashcard was *not* going to be my ticket out of Logan Square. My nicknames didn't exactly suggest drop-dead looks: "Perpetual Motion" (intense, wired energy); "Univac" (computer-like memory, A's in school); and "Braille Face" (that's right). . . . So with my brains, energy, and looks, I got the Personality flashcard.

> *—Marilu Henner recalling how her sisters' gifts differed from her own*

How are you, my sweet Tanyanka? I am often sad that you are not here with me. In spite of the fact that life is simply wonderful, things would be better still if I could hear your sweet nightingale voice, if I could sit and gossip with you as we used to do.... I haven't yet got quite used to things. It still seems strange to me that when I am at Yasnaya I am at home....

We didn't kiss each other often when we were together, but I am really going to do it this time. I send you a big kiss. Lyovochka [Tolstoy] wants to write to you and I must leave room for him.

I sign importantly, for the first time,

your sister,
Countess Sonya Tolstaya

September 28, 1862

—from a letter from Sonya Tolstoy to her sister Tanya

Janis and I went to the grocery store on Christmas Day to get cinnamon for the cookies we were making. We drove to the only place that was open. Janis and I were dressed for the festivities of the season, in long granny dresses. The streets were deserted, giving us a feeling of being the only people alive. Happy, loose, and carefree, we joked as we searched the aisles for our necessities. At the cash register I thought we took the checkout ladies' decorations in stride. How often do you see fifty-year-old women with their hair in French twists that have been sprayed with "snow" and have red Christmas balls stuck in carefully sculpted nests in their piled-high locks? We paid, and they snorted to each other about our long dresses and loose hair! We held in our howling laughter until the parking lot, then screamed, *"They're* laughing at *us?"*

> —*Laura Joplin writing about her sister, rock legend Janis Joplin*

Katerina and I are best friends. The only way we survived in this zoo was to stay close. . . . When I play Katerina, I pull harder for her than I do me. I've won all our matches, but I've suffered every time.

> —*Bulgarian tennis star Manuela Maleeva explaining in a 1990*
> *interview why she and her sister Katerina would enter different*
> *tournaments rather than face each other*

The Duchess of York wrote to Queen Mary: "We have decided to call our little daughter Margaret Rose. I hope you like it. I think that it is very pretty together." Princess Elizabeth liked it very much, and said, "I shall call her Bud."

"Why Bud?" asked Lady Cynthia Asquith, daughter-in-law of the King's first Prime Minister, to whom "Bud" probably sounded like American slang.

"Well, she's not a real Rose yet, is she? She's only a Bud."

—The future Queen Elizabeth, talking about her sister, Princess Margaret; quoted in The Queen *by Elizabeth Longford*

I am often with you, my dear Berthe. In my thoughts I follow you about in your studio, and wish that I could escape, were it only for a quarter of an hour, to breathe that air in which we lived for many years.

—Edma Pontillon writing to her fellow artist and beloved sister Berthe Morisot shortly after her marriage had separated the two for the first time

ISMENE: Can I not help you, even at this late hour?
ANTIGONE: Save your own life. I grudge you not your escape.
ISMENE: Alas! Can I not join you in your fate?
ANTIGONE: You cannot: you chose life, and I chose death.
ISMENE: But not without the warning that I gave you. . . .
ANTIGONE: Be comforted; you live, but I have given
   My life already, in service of the dead. . . .
ISMENE: But what is life to me without my sister?

> —*from Sophocles'* Antigone, *in which Antigone is condemned to death for burying their brother, and her sister Ismene cannot save her*

When the spring came, my sister Winifred was no longer ill. She was up, she was out, she looked as she had done before, her lovely hazel eyes and her long brown hair and her white skin were again luminous, she looked again like a girl in a painting. She would recite poetry to me for hours, she was glad to hold my hand and walk out with me, which was not the way of my eldest sister, the odious Lettie, who never touched me except to push me about, under the wounding pretext that in my stupidity, my slowness of sense, I was getting not in her way (that would make it seem as if she were looking to her own convenience in her irritation) but in the way of someone else who, almost inevitably, was purely imaginary. My sister Winifred only occasionally suggested that I was doing the wrong thing, and looking back over the best part of a century, I marvel at how a child so young could be so wise. She never corrected me, she simply supplied me with information regarding how things could be conveniently done, since it had not come my way.

Now I had someone to walk with who would pick me up if I fell and would pluck me back if I started to cross the road without making sure it was clear.

—Dame Rebecca West writing about her beloved sister Winifred

The popular conception of Lillian as soft and dreamy makes me think a little of the "gag" used too often in the comic strips. A hat lies upon the sidewalk; some person kicks it enthusiastically and finds to his astonishment and pain that there is hidden inside it a brick or flatiron.

Anyone who has tried kicking Lillian has discovered the solidity of that resistance. Life has stubbed its toe, often and often, trying to disorganize her stability. She remains steadfast, unshaken, imperturbable.

How I envy her the singleness of purpose, the indefatigability, the unabating seriousness which have taken her straight to the heights she has reached and will carry her on and on!. . . .

She is blessed with a constitution that can respond to any demand. Long after I am ready to be hauled off on a shutter, she, apparently so frail, can go on tirelessly, unruffled, cool and calm. That exquisite complexion of hers, that lovely lineless face—these she owes to her serenity, her unfailing poise. What a priceless combination for an artist! Unswerving ambition, deep seriousness of purpose, and not a nerve in her body!

. . . She is to me a never-ending source of astonishment and admiration. And I never cease to wonder at my luck in having for my sister the woman who, more than any other woman in America, possesses all the qualities of greatness.

—Dorothy Gish writing in Stage *magazine about her sister Lillian*

She is laughter, even on the cloudy days of life; nothing bothers her or saddens her or concerns her lastingly. Trouble gives only an evanescent shadow to her eyes and is banished with a shrug of a shoulder. . . .

She is the side of me that God left out. Her funny stories, her delight in sitting on men's hats, her ability to interest herself in a hundred and one people in whom she has not the slightest interest, her talent for quick and warm friendships, her philosophy of silver linings . . .

When Dorothy goes in swimming, she splashes the ocean into a beautifully gala muss; I just go in swimming. When she dances, there is no tomorrow; when I dance, the trombone always stubbornly reminds me of a director in a bad mood. . . .

The world to her is a big picnic with a great merry-go-round and lots of popcorn and wonderful balloons. All music, even the worst, seems so beautiful to her. All people amuse her. She even has fun getting her feet wet.

—Lillian Gish writing about her sister Dorothy

The best thing about having a sister was that I always had a friend.

Juli always stuck up for me. She was really good at fighting and always got the last word, so if someone was picking on me at school, she took care of it. The best time was the nighttime. We shared a room and would lie in bed and talk about everything. We'd play kissing games with our pillows and pretend they were boys we liked, and we'd lie with our heads upside down over the edge of the bed and laugh so hard—until Mom yelled that we'd better go to bed or else!

> —*Cali Rae Turner, actress and owner of* Call Cali, *talking about her sister Juli*

Dearest Jeanie,

Very many happy returns of the day. The day we turn 47 is a very significant day in our lives. So is the day we turn 48, I believe, but shall know more as to this next week. I am making a lot of new resolutions, such as to organise my life better, thus getting more done that I really think is worth doing, and not to mind being rude by leaving letters unwritten. It has taken me nearly 48 years to learn that both to answer letters and to do anything else in life without too much strain is impossible, so the letters (outside 3 or 4 people including the family) must go, and postcards take their place in future. Heaven grant me strength of mind to pursue this course! Or else I must keep a secretary, who will deal with correspondence. I hope you have made some equally useful plans....

Very much love,
Your loving twin, E.R.M.

—1924 birthday letter from novelist Rose Macaulay to her sister Jean, who was born less than a year after she was—hence the affectionate "twin"

I almost never got to be an actress or anything else because when I was a year and a half I was badly scalded. My mother had left me in my high chair with one of my sisters to take care of me. Someone rang the doorbell and while my sister was gone I reached across, dragged a pot off the stove, and spilled the boiling liquid all over my arm. Grandma Darragh took me home to live with her after that and I stayed until I was ten.

My sister Hazel used to come over and play with me. We're very close. In fact sometimes people, meeting Hazel, become a little glassy-eyed and mutter, "Oh, no, not *two* of them!" Hazel is the funniest girl in the world. All we used to have to do was hold up a finger at each other and we'd both howl with laughter.

Hazel was always wanting to teach me something. She wanted me to learn the Highland fling and the sword dance so I'd get a prize at the Scottish dances. I'd stall Hazel. "I'll learn if you'll play jacks with me first," I'd say. So she'd play jacks. "Now, just play ball with me once and then I'll learn." So Hazel would join me in banging the ball against the door and in nothing flat Grandma would appear wanting to know why all the noise with our uncle resting.

—*Gracie Allen on her sister and childhood performing partner Hazel*

We had a couple of fantasies that we shared. One time we were pretending to be Mary and Madine Slickery, these two characters in our dream world ... Madine had something like one hundred children, that they called the Slickery children. I was Madine and Suzie was Mary. They would move all over the world building castles, and they could build them very fast because there were so many Slickery children; each one would take a brick, and that's how fast it would get done. I loved castles. We used to play that endlessly in the dining room.

> —*Anne Rice describing a favorite game she played with her sister Alice, who was called Suzie*

On the drive to the church, Mamma sits with Anna on the back seat of the drosky. Gerda and I, as usual, sit with our backs to the horses. But today I am not sorry to ride backward, for in this way I can look at Anna the whole time.

But it is not at her dress I am looking, nor at the filigree brooch she received from Mamma as a confirmation gift. I am looking into her eyes.

They are large soulful eyes of a greyish-brown, with perhaps a tinge of olive. However, it is not their color that I see, but their expression of serene expectancy. I should love to know what it is that she expects. It seems to me as though she were standing outside the iron gate of some great and glorious castle and longing to be let in to see the beautiful rooms, the broad staircases, and the vaulted ceilings.

Somehow I feel certain that her wish will be granted. Before long the gate will open and a handsome young prince, dressed in satin and velvet, will come out and bow low to Anna, saying that he is Count Bernhard Bertelskold and bid her welcome to Majniemi Castle.

But Anna will not look at him or take his proferred hand, nor will she pass through the gate; for Anna does not stand outside Majniemi Castle; she stands at the gate of heaven waiting to see God and His angels.

—*Selma Lagerlof, novelist, writing about her sister Anna*

"This here is Faith," she says, introducing her sister. "This is Hope. Say hello, Hope. I'm Charity.

"And you know," she says, pausing for dramatic effect, "the greatest of these is Charity!" Yes, she's used the line plenty of times before, but her face still crinkles as she guffaws.

—*Charity Cardwell Lawson, one of the three oldest living triplets, citing her favorite sisterly joke in a* New York Times *interview*

When I look at Martha today, I see parts of myself and parts of my history. She has tested and helped me as no other person has, making me understand my limitations and my capacity for generosity. She is also my only immediate link to a life that is, for the most part, buried. We understand each other in a special way that defies the empathy of well-meaning friends. Whatever happens, we will be there to remind each other where we have been and how far we have come.

—*Barbara Lovenheim, journalist, writing about her younger sister Martha*

I looked on her as a mother, and I worshipped the ground she trod on. She would look after me and comfort me and be firm when I had my tantrums. I loved her as a child and I loved her all her life. During holidays she would write out a prayer from her prayer book for me every night. I have them still and can remember them, like "Jesu tender shepherd hear me/bless thou little lamb tonight; through the darkness be thou near me/ keep me safe till morning light...." And then it would end "For Mary from Edwina" and the date. If Edwina was away for a few days when she came home she would say, "Darling—did you say the little prayer?"

> —Mary Ashley, *later Lady Delamere, speaking of her adored elder sister, Edwina, later Countess Mountbatten and the last vicereine of India*

My sister and I are 11 years apart, so basically she was like having a baby of my own. I diapered her, fed her, and was there like a proud parent for every step of her development.

> —Melissa Gilbert *on raising her little sister, actress Sara Gilbert*

When someone came to the house, they would bring two dolls, one for Grace and one for me. My dolls got to be an absolute disgrace because we'd both play with mine. Grace kept hers safely away. Years later, when I visited the palace, I looked into her closet and saw all her old dolls. I said, "My God, Grace, you still have those dolls?" And she said, "Don't you still have your dolls?" I said, "No, we destroyed mine playing with them."

—*Lizanne (Elizabeth Ann) Kelly on her sister Grace (later Princess of Monaco)*

There were three of us Skirvin children. I'm the oldest, then comes my sister, Marguerite, and my brother, William. We are not a bit alike. Marguerite, who is now Mrs. George Tyson and lives in Nevada, is blond and blue-eyed—the real beauty of the family. She is of an artistic nature, and is never happier than when in the midst of decorating a house. Marguerite likes the formal way of doing things and is much more proper than I am—sometimes I think she is a little shocked at me when I dance all night or badger a senator for his vote on women's rights. She has great tact, and when we are together she helps to keep me from letting my temper flare up, which it does on occasion. . . . Marguerite loves to read books, has great powers of concentration, and is an expert at bridge. Canasta is more my speed, and I never can find the time to read. I like to get my information from talking to people and watching things happen.

—*Perle Mesta, renowned Washington hostess, on her sister Marguerite*

We had violent fights and a fierce, blind devotion to each other. There was no question we would both go into show business. It came with Mum's milk: you will be a star.

Toni was a huge star in Australia. People always wanted me to sing her hits. An announcer once introduced me, "Here she is . . . I don't remember her name but she's Toni Lamond's sister."

> —*Helen Reddy recalling her early relationship with her older half sister Toni*

Mary had aspirations, confidence, and a will to succeed like no other. While I wallowed in my troubles, making long lists of life's injustices, Mary operated with great practicality and logic. When we moved from one house to another to reduce the mortgage payments, it was Mary who had the necessary resourcefulness to make the move tolerable, even fun. Mary was the one who found a house with lots of windows and a cheerful ambience. And it was Mary who got the best price from the moving company, and who finally managed to extract from me a smile as we entered the new house, declaring, "Ah, Paradise. . . ."

> —*Marti Leimbach, novelist, writing about her sister Mary*

To be given a glimpse into the radiant mysteries of the Medical Book was a reward for good behavior. On such days, my older sister Ruth and I were treated to a graphically unfolding diagram of the physiology of a woman, in which successive leaves were folded back to reveal the muscles, nerves, blood vessels, that lay underneath. On some rare occasions, when we had been supremely good children, the last leaves of the chart were folded back, and my sister and I would exclaim rapturously over "the dear little baby" at the bottom of the diagram, waiting to be born.

> —*Margaret Bourke-White, photographer, recalling how she and her sister Ruth learned the facts of life*

The difference between us is I will shop for something expensive but just buy one thing, say, a nice little blue suit from Valentino. Whereas Alex will buy 150 shirts and 150 cardigans for $200 [each], thinking she's pulled off a great bargain. But they just sit there and accumulate and accumulate.

> —*Marie-Chantal Miller (recently wed to Crown Prince Pavlos of Greece) explaining how she and her sister Alex (recently wed to Prince Alexandre von Furstenberg), shop for clothes*

"You're my proof, Connie. You were there. God knows they were miserable years, but imagine if we'd each been there alone."

Connie looks away, her wrists warming where Faith holds them. "Sometimes I think we *were* there alone, nothing more to do with each other than two little hamsters in a cage."

Faith drags her palms over her wet cheeks. "But Connie, imagine being *one* little hamster in a cage."

All at once, the memory of a high-up room: a hotel room, with flimsy carpets and vinyl chairs and a strange city throbbing outside the windows. Connie tries to picture this room without Faith in it—Faith, slung over the couch reading a book, or standing by the window gazing into the street, or examining the directions for a toy from Armand. She sees herself alone with the avocado drapes, the pale food from the next-door restaurant, the paintings of daisies, the sounds in the hall. For a moment she longs to go all the way back there, to feel herself a child again with a sister who accompanied her, silent but steadfast, through the steely corridor of childhood; she longs to go back for the click of times it would take to thank Faith for existing. For bearing witness.

Exhausted, she slides into Faith's lap, soothed by the gentle pressure of her sister's cool hand on her forehead. "Faith," she murmurs. "You're my one decent memory."

—*from* Secret Language *by Monica Wood*

I have been married to Dick for 25 years now, and have been "married" to Peggy, Kathy, and Janet for thirty—and, living with them for almost forty!

We have supported each other through good times and bad, for richer or poorer, in sickness and health, yet we have all gone our separate ways, each standing on her own two feet and living her personal life according to her singular beliefs. I admire all three of them for the good women they are—both in mind and spirit. They each have characteristics that I would like to take from. Peg has an ability to put to memory every bit of knowledge she acquires, and yet she is not pompous. Kath has a very simple way of expressing her feelings and is not afraid to do it. And Jan is a person who is very willing to make an effort to change with the times.

They are good wives, and I would "marry" them all over again. I thank God for selecting three very special people to be with me ... "till death do us part."

> —*Dianne Lennon writing about her three younger sisters, Kathy, Peggy, and Janet, who performed with her as the Lennon Sisters*

From the time we were babies, Janet—just three years my junior—and I were the world's best pals. When a couple of girls can share Hoot Gibson and Tim McCoy days, and make up songs to talk to one another, their bond is unbroken. Those days passed away too quickly. Janet and I have also shared adult experiences, both of comfort and discomfort. Happy feelings, or those of emotional pain, have held us, strongly tied, through many trials.

I always found Dee Dee the quiet guide, the helpful companion and friend. With Peggy, I think a deeper friendship came as we grew older. For all of us, being together, singing together brought the true closeness, the oneness that melded us one into another. It is our public image, that oneness. It's natural. We bring it from our home!

> —*Kathy Lennon, writing about the sisters who share her life onstage and off*

How do I feel about my Sisters?
They love me; they know me and they still love me.
I'd love to be skinny for Kathy. I'd love to be more
Quiet like Deed. I'd love to be able to handle my
Home like Janet. They are my best friends. They are
Me.

> —*Peggy Lennon on her sisters and singing partners, Kathy, Dianne, and Janet*

To Dee Dee—for braiding my hair all of those years and putting up with my fussiness at having to look perfect; for being my shining example of graciousness and composure. When I was little I thought of her as a Sister Superior, and I would never disagree or contradict her, out of respect for her position. Somewhere along the way, though, I grew up, and we became peers. Now I consider her one of my best friends and confidantes. I would very much love to have her face and hair, and her golf swing.

To Peggy—for coming to my rescue when I was pressed for time, and writing a poem for me that won me an "A" from my fourth-grade teacher. For being my example of holiness. I can remember looking at her when we were in church together and thinking she would ascend to heaven at any moment; and later, sharing motherhood hints, carpools, and life philosophies. I wish I had her big brown eyes and big smart brain (and her skill in making stuffed manicotti).

To Kathy—for being my best pal my whole life. For our childhood years of sharing every thought, experience, and cute outfit. (Although I do wish she hadn't shared with me her discovery that there was no Santa Claus. I was only five.) For double dates, more support than I deserved, and for being there during my most traumatic times. She still takes care of me, and I still let her. I would give anything to have her singing voice, her small waist, and her self-confidence.

> —*Janet Lennon writing in appreciation of her three sisters and singing partners*

I had grown even more timid, shrinking and sensitive in the presence of others; absurdly careful and methodical for a child; afraid of giving trouble by letting my wants be known, thereby giving the very pain I sought to avoid, and instead of feeling that my freedom gave me time for recreation or play, it seemed to me like time wasted, and I looked anxiously about for some useful occupation.

As usual, my blessed sister, Mrs. Vassall, came to the rescue. Taking advantage of an all-absorbing love of poetry (which I always had) she made a weapon of it by providing me with the poetical works of Walter Scott, which I had not read, and proposed that we read them together. We naturally commenced with "The Lady of the Lake." I was immediately transported to the Highlands and the Bonnie Braes, plucking the heather and the broom and guiding the skiff across Loch Katrine, listening to the sweet warning song of poor crazed Blanche of Devon, thrilling with, "Saxon, I am Roderick Dhu," and trudging along with the old minstrel and Ellen to Sterling tower and the Court of Fitz-James. "Marmion" followed, and then all the train of English poetry that a child could take in.

> —*Clara Barton recalling how her beloved sister introduced her, a frail, solitary child, to the wonders of literature*

My sister is a photographer of things, I of people. She loves French and the linguistic side of her foreign-language education. I always loathed the grammar and vocabulary drills but loved the fiction and poetry. She is an optimist, I a fatalist, although she sees these traits reversed in us. She drinks her coffee black; my first cup must have milk and sugar. I am five feet eight and have the build of Nana; she is five-two and structurally resembles Grandma and my aunt. Apart from these differences and in spite of the five years that separate us, we are very much the same. I don't think we look alike, but barbers claim our heads have the same shape, and once a perfect stranger accosted me on a train and asked me if I was the sister of her friend.

—*Gayle Pemberton, professor and memoirist, reflecting on her sister in "None of the Above"*

Jon had always had the power to terrify. She had a strange dark macabre streak in her that at times made her another person. As a child she could terrify, particularly me; other children used to beg their mothers, "*Please* need we go to tea with the Goddens?"

We used to make them play a game called Iurki in our big nursery, dark when its shutters were closed. The luckless children were compelled to build a tower putting a chair on our sturdy table, a stool on the chair, and then climbed up to the top of a massive wardrobe. The guest children would be induced to climb up, the stool, chair, and table were taken away so that none could get down; the lights were turned off and one of us who had stayed behind would come in as a ghost.

When it was Jon it was blood-curdling; something soft with moving ends would brush our cheeks; "Spider," crooned Jon—cut wool on the end of a fishing rod, "Big spider. Black Widow spider. Poison. Poison." A hooka pipe wet and sinuous would come with a hiss. "Cobra. Cobra," and a white shrouded faceless ghost would moan, "I've got no nose. No nose." Some of the children had hysterics. "*Please* need we go to the Goddens?"

—Rumer Godden writing about childhood with her novelist sister Jon

Having a sister is like having a best friend you can't get rid of. You know whatever you do, they'll still be there. We work together as a partnership, and pull together. You know she won't sabotage the company or run off with all the money. Whatever happens, though, even if the partnership should fail, we'll still be sisters. It's easy enough to share a flat with a friend, but working with them? I wouldn't want to try that!

—Amy Li, who runs a design firm with her sister Grace

We were all, brothers and sisters alike, healthy and strong, vigorous and active; our appetites were curtailed only through necessity. We played the same games together and shared the same sports—baseball, skating, swimming, hunting. Nevertheless, except that we all had red hair, shading from carrot to bronze, we were sharply distinct physically. The girls were small and feminine, the boys husky and brawny. When I went out in the world and observed men, otherwise admirable, who could not pound a nail or use a saw, pick, shovel, or ax, I was dumfounded. I had always taken for granted that any man could make things with his hands.

I expected this even of women. My oldest sister, Mary, possessed, more than the rest of us, an innate charm and gentleness. She could do anything along domestic lines—embroidery, dress making, tailoring, cooking; she could concoct the most delicious and unusual foods, and mix delicate pastries. But she was also an expert at upholstering, carpentry, painting, roofing with shingles or with thatch. When Mary was in the house, we never had to send for a plumber. She rode gracefully and handled the reins from the carriage seat with equal dexterity; she could milk a cow and deliver a baby; neighbors called her to tend their sick cattle, or, when death came, to lay out the body; she tutored in mathematics and Latin, and was well-read in the classics; yet she liked most the theater, and was a dramatic critic whose judgment was often sought. In all that she did her sweetness and dearness were apparent, though she performed her many kindnesses in secret.

—*Margaret Sanger, women's health pioneer, recalling how her sister Mary's gifts inspired her*

Had I died,—in what peculiar misery should I have left you, my nurse, my friend, my sister!—You, who had seen all the fretful selfishness of my latter days; who had known all the murmurings of my heart!—How should I have lived in *your* remembrance!—My mother too! How could you have consoled her!—I cannot express my own abhorrence of myself.—Whenever I looked towards the past, I saw some duty neglected, or some failing indulged. Every body seemed injured by me. . . . But you,—you above all, above my mother, who had been wronged by me. I, and only I, knew your heart and its sorrows; yet, to what did it influence me?—not to any compassion that could benefit you or myself.—Your example was before me: but to what avail?—Was I more considerate of you and your comfort? Did I imitate your forbearance, or lessen your restraints . . . No;—not less when I knew you to be unhappy, than when I had believed you at ease, did I turn away from every exertion of duty or friendship; scarcely allowed sorrow to exist but with me, regretting only *that* heart which had deserted and wronged me, and leaving you for whom I professed an unbounded affection, to be miserable for my sake.

> —*Marianne Dashwood reproving herself for hurting her sister,*
> *Elinor, in* Sense and Sensibility *by Jane Austen*

One of my greatest joys was reading, or pretending to read, the few newspapers, magazines, and books that were available in our home. These were, for the most part, books Elizabeth had purchased for the few college semesters she could finance. She taught me to read when I was five, and although Shakespeare was beyond me, I would "read" the pictures, lying flat on my stomach with the heavy volumes spread out on the floor. Milton's *Paradise Lost*, a huge book with beautiful pictures, fascinated and scared me. If I asked her, Elizabeth would tell me the stories. Later, when I played alone, I would tell my dolls the stories in my own words. My mother, always practical and compelled by circumstances to be tough, was not a reader. She strictly forbade her children to read trash, and any paperback was trash to her. She frowned on the popular comic book of that day, "Peck's Bad Boy," but Kirby and I loved it. As I grew older, no rule against reading could stop me. I hid *Three Weeks* and *Tempest and Sunshine* on the top of our big privy under the plum tree in our orchard and read them until Mother's fretful call returned me to the house. . . . When I was six, I told Elizabeth, then twenty, "I'm going to write my own 'Peck's Bad Boy' when I grow up." Always supportive, she assured me that I would.

—*Bess Whitehead Scott, first woman reporter on* The Houston Post *city desk, circa 1915, on her older sister Elizabeth*

"Why, Ann Eliza!" Evelina stood transfixed by the sight of the parcel beside her plate.

Ann Eliza, tremulously engaged in filling the teapot, lifted a look of hypocritical surprise.

"Sakes, Evelina! What's the matter?"

The younger sister had rapidly untied the string, and drawn from its wrappings a round nickel clock of the kind to be bought for a dollar-seventy-five.

"Oh, Ann Eliza, how could you?" She set the clock down and the sisters exchanged agitated glances across the table.

"Well," the elder retorted, "*ain't* it your birthday?"

"Yes, but—"

"Well, and ain't you had to run round the corner to the Square every morning, rain or shine, to see what time it was, ever since we had to sell mother's watch last July? Ain't you, Evelina?"

"Yes, but—"

"There ain't any buts. We've always wanted a clock and now we've got one: that's all there is about it. Ain't she a beauty, Evelina?" Ann Eliza, putting back the kettle on the stove, leaned over her sister's shoulder to pass an approving hand over the circular rim of the clock.

—*from* The Bunner Sisters *by Edith Wharton*

The Bridge was open last night as we came through, in a storm of rain, a sailing ship passing, and all very romantic, and as usual I thought of you. Do you think we have the same pair of eyes, only different spectacles? I rather think I'm more nearly attached to you than sisters should be. Why is it I never stop thinking of you, even when walking in the marsh this afternoon . . . If you notice a dancing light on the water, that is me. The light kisses your nose, then your eyes, and you can't rub it off; my darling honey how I adore you, and lord knows I can't say what it means to me to come into the room and find you sitting there.

—*Virginia Woolf writing to her sister Vanessa Bell in a letter dated August 17, 1937*

My Billy,

I have been for the last 3 days completely submerged in "The Waves"—and am left rather gasping, out of breath, choking, half-drowned, as you might expect. I must read it again when I may hope to float more quietly, but meanwhile I'm so overcome by the beauty . . . it's impossible not to tell you or give you some hint of what's been happening to me. For it's quite as real an experience as having a baby or anything else, being moved as you have succeeded in moving me.

—*Vanessa Bell, painter, writing to her sister Virginia Woolf about her work, in a letter dated October 15?, 1931*

My parents and the other eight children tried to include Rose in everything we did. At Hyannis Port I would take her as crew in our boat races, and I remember that she usually could do what she was told. She was especially helpful with the jib, and she loved to be in the winning boat. Winning at anything always brought a smile to her face. . . .

She loved compliments. Every time I would say, "Rose, you have the best teeth and smile in the family," she would smile for hours.

—Eunice Kennedy Shriver writing about her sister Rosemary, who helped inspire her commitment to Special Olympics

So Barbara and Hilary set up house together—Harriet and Belinda—in their thirties still and not their fifties as Barbara had foretold ten years before. They had always got on well. When they were children, Barbara was very protective of her younger sister, but as they grew up the roles were reversed, and it was Hilary, more and more, who took the lead. . . .

"It is marvellous being with Hilary," Barbara had written in 1938, "we have the most wonderful jokes about everything." They went on having wonderful jokes together for the rest of their lives.

—Hazel Holt, biographer and literary executor, on Barbara Pym and her sister Hilary, who lived together most of their lives

MELANIE: *(kissing Scarlett)* Scarlett, I thought of you at *our* wedding yesterday and hoped yours would be as beautiful. And it was.
SCARLETT: *(like a sleepwalker)* Was it?
MELANIE: *(nods emphatically)* Now we're really and truly sisters.

> —*From the screenplay of* Gone With the Wind

I have not been really in spirits, nor had one natural laugh, since I lost you; . . . I know not, in truth, whether I most miss you when happy or when sad. That I wish for you most when happy is certain; but that nothing upon earth can do so much good, when sad, as your society, is certain too.

> —*Fanny Burney, 18th-century novelist, writing to her younger sister Susanna two years after her sister's marriage*

Deborah came in last, but she never stopped swimming. She swam and swam—the race had been over for five minutes, and she was still swimming. She wasn't gonna win the race, but she was gonna finish it. And when she did finish, the poor child had to be dragged out of the water by the vice-principal. Everybody was cheering—I think they cheered more for her than they did for the winner—because she kept going. And Debbie has always been like that.

—Phylicia Rashad talking about her sister Debbie Allen

The age difference between us is five years, so that in our youth, there was more that separated us than brought us together. Yet both of us grew up in the "sisterhood is powerful" era of the late 60s and early 70s so that as adults we began to form a friendship that was based on family ties but nourished by the reality that even if we were not related we would choose to spend time together.

In 1990, when we were both "between" jobs, we decided to start our own business, a newspaper syndication service. We called our business Sisters Syndicate. As the business caught on, it gave us the opportunity and the excuse to get together frequently, even though we live in different cities.

We've been able to be together for the important events of each other's lives, from the birth of Christine's four children to the publication of Lee's first book. Outside the business we still have fun doing the things we did thirty years ago—rummaging in each other's closets, swapping jewelry, going out to eat, and comparing notes on our love lives. We never tire of each other's company, and even go on vacations together.

Our original goal for Sisters Syndicate was to make it a business success. But we have achieved so much more because the business has enabled us to build a special relationship with each other.

Friends, partners, and sisters. What more could we want?

—*Andrea Lee Negroni, attorney, and Lorie Christine Negroni, journalist*

[A] very early memory: I am walking in a field with my elder sister, and we are gathering flowers. She picked a clover and told me it was good to eat. So I pulled off the petals one by one, imitating her, and bit off the white part inside, which was most delicious. Another time, probably a year or two later, I remember we were trying to catch a squirrel. For a long time it kept us running as it skipped from one tree to another. Eventually I climbed a tree to frighten the squirrel down and by some miracle my sister caught it and was bitten on her hand so that it bled. Perhaps it was because of this that I was called Squirrel. . . .

> —*Dame Marie Rambert, ballerina and founder of Ballet Rambert, writing about her sister*

I think you are perfectly right to go on & get a position if you can; it is what I am going to do as soon as I am able. I do not believe in living in this poor half-starving way. Poverty & dependence crushes every noble feeling out of the heart. I do not think it lowers a woman to work for her living, on the contrary it shows courage & perseverance. . . . Sis, we are destined for something—there is no use to think otherwise, either good or bad. As for me I would not be surprised to find myself in 20 years from now either in the penitentiary or on the throne of England. . . . I must do something. I must be something.

> —*Nina King writing to her sister, Grace King, Reconstruction-era Louisiana writer*

She used to have a doll stove—a real cooking stove for kids—and she'd make us itty bitty cakes and cookies and goodies on it, and of course I ate them. She'd plan games for us and she'd give plays, too. She made up one where I was Raggedy Ann—it was performed at the Miller Theater—and she made all the backdrops and scenery and designed the costumes, too. At home she had her own tiny theater—just about the size of an apple box. She painted beautiful little paper figures and waltzed them around and told stories, and all the neighborhood kids would come and watch.

—*June Brooks recalling her sister, 1920s film star Louise Brooks*

As a young child, my tendency was to emulate my big sister. Angela, of course, was always treating me like a little sister. However, we developed a very, very close relationship with each other. You don't have to be the sister of Angela Davis to appreciate her intellect. But a real advantage for me is that I get to talk to her probably more than other people do about what concerns her most. I learn from her experiences and from her thinking.

—*Sonya Davis, lawyer, reminiscing about her sister, activist and professor Angela Davis*

The reason we get along so well is our years of practice. I credit our parents. We weren't allowed to argue. When we did, we were punished. Not one, but two or all three of us, so we'd pull together.

—Louise Mandrell on her sisters Barbara and Irlene

I feel about my sisters the way a mother feels about her children. You don't mess with the momma lion.

—Barbara Mandrell on her sisters Louise and Irlene

My sister Mary—best friend, soul mate, business partner—inspires me, awes me, encourages me. She is the first person I turn to in times of trouble, in times of joy. We've always been close but the death of our mother in 1986 made us inseparable. We moved to different cities after college, but soon discovered we couldn't bear to be apart, and so Mary joined me in Washington. We now own a business together, and I couldn't be happier.

The only thing that annoys me about Mary is that she's always right. But that's also what I love about her. She always gives it to me straight. Though we work together and live 3 blocks apart, we must speak at least twice a day on the phone. My boyfriend and her husband just don't get it. We do—we're sisters.

—*Stephanie Abbajay, owner (with her sister Mary) of Washington, D.C.'s Toledo Lounge*

My sister and I are only one year apart, so growing up we used to have terrible fights. But we also had two older brothers who used to love to pick on us. We learned very early that by uniting our forces we would be a tough target. Thus we were able to instantly set aside our differences (which, because we were children, were always childish ones) in order to conquer the larger danger at hand—our bigger, meaner brothers! Since our parents thought it best that the "kids settled their own differences," we learned to rely on each other thoroughly. Even if we were fighting, we knew the other would be there in a moment if the need arose.

As we grew older, the bond deepened. We rarely fight now, unless we have a disagreement about the business we own and run together. We survived several family tragedies, including the deaths of our mother and one of our brothers. Most people are disturbed and awed by how close Stephanie and I are now. She is my sister, my best friend, sometimes my mother, always my confidant, my touchstone, my idol, my light, and my sunshine. My life would be dark without her.

> *—Mary Abbajay writing about her sister Stephanie, with whom she owns and runs Washington, D.C.'s Toledo Lounge*

Often as we grew older, Ward and his best friend Jess would go off fishing or setting "cat" hooks, and Elizabeth and I would play "playhouse" up on the rock cliffs. We gathered armfuls of green moss and spread it for rugs on our floors. We made little chairs and sofas of rocks and spread these. Then we would serve tea in acorn cups and saucers, talk "lady talk," and wear decorated hats. Elizabeth was the town "milliner," and we would gather a big weed leaf that grew nearby, called hatweed, about as big as a rhubarb leaf and about that droopy shape. Elizabeth would fasten the hat leaves together in the back with a sharp thorn and decorate them with hillside flowers, the ones her "customers" used for money: oxeye daisies, black-eyed Susans, wild roses, and pink milkweed bloom.

In late summer, when the long, delicate green milkweed pods were full, we would strip off the outer pods and carefully take out the silky white insides. These were our "milkweed ladies," as pure and delicate as soft white dove-birds, there on our rock cliff in the sun. We would invite them to "tea," a crowded three of them sitting so ladylike on our moss sofa; and we, in our millinery hats, serving them. We would tell them in high-pitched Southern voices, about the Ladies' Aid meetings and the strawberry festival down at the church; and one day I made up a rhyme:

> Milkweed ladies so fair and fine,
> Won't you have a sip of my columbine?
> Or a thimble of thimbleberry wine?

As we talked and laughed, the golden finches that frequented the thickets flashed back and forth, and their gold and black wings caught the slants of sun.

—Louise McNeill, poet, recalling how she and her sister Elizabeth created a world of their own

Occasionally Unity and I united in the forbidden sport of "teasing Debo." The teasing had to be done well out of earshot of my father, as Debo was his prime favorite, and fearful consequences could follow if we made her cry. She was an extraordinarily softhearted child, and it was easy to make her huge blue eyes brim with tears. . . .

Unity invented a tragic story involving a Pekingese puppy. "The telephone bell rang," it went. "Grandpa got up from his seat and went to answer it. 'Lill ill!' he cried . . ." Lill was on her deathbed, a victim of consumption. Her dying request was that Grandpa should care for her poor little Pekingese. However, in all the excitement of the funeral, the peke was forgotten, and was found several days later beside his mistress's grave, dead of starvation and a broken heart.

This story never failed to send Debo into paroxysms of grief, no matter how often it was retold. Naturally, we were severely punished for telling it. Months of allowance would be confiscated, and often we were sent to bed as well. A more borderline case would be merely to say, in tones fraught with tragedy, "THE TELE-PHONE BELL RANG," in which case Debo howled as loudly as if we had told the story to its bitter end.

—Jessica Mitford, writer, on her sisters Unity and Debo

My sister and I have a very close bond and are the best of friends. We are identical twin veterinarians and own the Sisters Veterinary Clinic in Sisters, Oregon. (The town, which sits at the base of the Three Sisters mountains, gave the clinic its name, not us.)

The very best thing about my sister is the way we work together. We both have the same love for animals and the same practice philosophy. I trust her with my patients and I work well with her as a surgery partner. If an emergency arises, she'll be there. We do a lot of brainstorming trying to figure out the best treatment or the best technique for some of the more challenging cases.

One time I was especially grateful to my sister during a Sunday emergency. It was a dog with a large hernia. The dog was in a lot of pain and I had to begin the surgery immediately. I soon found that there were more problems than I had anticipated. I needed a second pair of hands to save the dog, and just then my sister walked in. Driving through town, she'd been curious why my car was at the clinic. I was so happy to see her. With her enthusiastic help, we saved the dog.

Another emergency involved a dog with a large hemorrhaging tumor who needed a blood transfusion and surgery immediately. I called my sister for help. She even brought her own dog for a blood donor. We worked quickly as a team, each knowing what the other was thinking. The dog recovered beautifully.

No matter what life brings, happy times or sad times, we are always there for each other.

—*Sharon Sharpnack, veterinarian and twin, writing about her sister and partner Susan Conner*

I feel very fortunate to have a close friend who is also my sister. Our relationship is extra special because we are identical twins. We think alike, we have similar feelings, and we tend to react to situations in the same way, so it's easy for us to understand and be sympathetic to each other.

When we were growing up, we always played together. We even had our own secret language that no one but our mother could understand. It's been difficult to find someone I could really be close to and who would give me the kind of unconditional love I found with my sister, my mother, and the dogs I have owned. I thought I'd found it with the man I married, but he'd been raised an only child and didn't know how to communicate, how to share or be considerate of others' feelings. Maybe my marriage was a disappointment because I was looking for a perfect relationship like the one I have with my sister.

When we entered junior high, the teachers decided to separate us into different classes. We did not want to be split up and couldn't understand why our parents agreed to it. One time we switched all of our classes so we could see what each other's teachers were like. It was sort of scary because I didn't know if I could remember where Sharon sat in each class. I think one of the six teachers suspected, and gave us a surprise algebra quiz. Luckily, I got an A on the test for my sister!

—*Susan Conner, veterinarian, writing about her sister and fellow vet Sharon Sharpnack*

Many thanks dear for your jolly letter but I wish you hadn't ended in such a melancholy way. Surely you don't imagine if *I* was married I should let you be a governess. You would have to put your independent spirit in your pocket & come & live with me. If we quarreled you could go & stay with Nina for a few days & then (I speak from experience) no sooner you were gone than I should want you back again.

> —*Beatrice, later renowned British actress Mrs. Patrick Campbell, writing to her sister Lulo*

Dixie was my idol. I adored her. I loved all my sisters, but I was closest to Dixie because we were closer in age, and we were the only two left at home after Frances, Virginia, and Mary married and moved away.

Dixie was seven years older than I and she started dating when I was about eight, a very impressionable age. We slept in the same room in the same bed, and she always woke me up when she came in from a date. We'd lie there and whisper and giggle with the dying firelight flickering against the bedroom walls, and I thought she was the neatest thing that ever was. I wanted to be just like her. I copied her in every way I could. When she started wearing makeup and bobbed her hair and got her first bra I couldn't wait to do the same. I watched every move she made. Those were the days of short dresses and flapper clothes, Dixieland jazz and the Charleston—the height of the Roaring Twenties—and Dixie was Thoroughly Modern Millie. She was a swinger, but she was good. She didn't do anything wrong—none of us did—but she loved to date and dance and dart around in open-top cars with boys in raccoon coats. I remember when she was dating the high school football star and he gave her his letter sweater with three stripes on the arm. Oh, how I wanted to grow up *quick* so I could get a letter sweater, too!

—*Ophelia Colley Cannon, better known as country comedienne Minnie Pearl, reminiscing about her sister Dixie*

My sister, Jerry Martin Andrews, loves everybody, just like Dolly Levi, and she is also the con woman of all time. She gets people together, she gets them engaged, she gets them married, and all the time they think that *they* thought of it. And they all love her forever. She's quite a dame, my sister, and me playing *her*, as Dolly, [in *Hello, Dolly*] was one of the high spots of my career.

—Mary Martin writing about her sister Jerry

The first thing I can remember loving was Manya . . . She was a quiet child, sitting quietly, hugging her furry rabbit. She had a heart-shaped face with big brown eyes and the loveliest colouring of red and brown and such pretty limbs. Her little arms and legs of just the right firmness of flesh. I loved the perfection of her and felt responsible for her. When the French nurse put her for punishment in the cellar, I could not bear the thought of Manya in the dark down there and I stood at the top of the kitchen stairs and yelled with all my might. The whole household came running and Manya had to be released.

—Frieda von Richthofen, later Mrs. D. H. Lawrence, writing about her sister

I was the baby for eleven years, then Vanessa was born. I've got four sisters, and they are all so different. We're close, but not really "in-your-face" close. All my sisters are half sisters, and all our lives we've been available for each other. It's understood: all you've got to do is ask—and we'll all come running.

My oldest sister, Joyce, was always considered Mama's favorite, but all along *it's been me*. I'm her favorite. This is a big fight for us trying to figure out who Mama loves the most.

> —*Loretta Devine, actress, on her sisters Joyce, Marolin, Carolin, and Vanessa*

My sister Pamela decided early on she was going to turn herself into a very glamorous person. She had a lot of ambition. When our parents would have people to tea and dinner, it was Pamela who always begged to be allowed to sit at the table while I was so shy I hid in the nursery.

> —*Sheila Digby Moore talking about her sister Pamela Digby Roosevelt Hayward Harriman, current U.S. Ambassador to France*

Having a little sister is having a built-in playmate (and fan club, although you don't realize or appreciate it at the time). And when, many years later, she reminded me of some advice I had given her when I was in college that she had followed, I realized the awesome power and responsibility wielded by the older sister. She'd *treasured* what I said, listened to the advice, and remembered it years later; I didn't think anyone paid any attention to anything I ever said!

I remember the first time I wrote her a letter—she must have been at camp—and I wrote, "Dear Abby." It was so odd, like writing to the newspaper column, not my sister. I have since gotten over that.

My sister gives me the best funky brooches. When I get dressed up in my serious lawyer suits, it is important to pin a pink polka-dotted wooden fish on my lapel to make it clear who I really am. In the end, despite our sometime differences, we know who the other is, and even knowing that—the best and the worst—love each other.

—*Sally R. Zanger, lawyer, writing about her sister Abby Zanger, Ph.D., Harvard University professor*

Now that she must see for Mary as well as for herself, Laura saw everything—the way the wind bent the grass, the way the land rose to meet the sky, the way the sky seemed lit by a strange luminescence. Only at the far edge of the prairie could she see a faint pale band of blue.

Necessity had sharpened her perceptions, and she struggled for words to express them. When she saw a white horse and a rider and the sun come together where the rim of the prairie touched the sky, she saw more than a man and his horse and the red blazing sun. She saw something wild and free and beautiful. When she tried to tell Mary about it, she felt how poor words were for telling what she had seen. She tried to find the right words, but there were some things that couldn't be fitted into words.

> —*from* Laura: The Life of Laura Ingalls Wilder *about the writer and her beloved sister Mary, who went blind as a young girl*

As for Louisa, I really think that in my life I never knew or heard of anything equal to the sweetness and gentleness of her disposition. She is indeed as yet quite an angel. She is mildness itself. It is not in nature to ruffle the sweetness of her temper one single instant.

One may say of her as Lord Hastings does in the play of Jane Shore,

> *Without one jarring atom was she formed*
> *and gentleness and joy made up her being*

which I think is the prettiest character that can be given any woman.

—*Emily Lennox, great-granddaughter of Charles II, describing her sister Louisa in a letter to a friend c. 1750s*

The note from my sister was short and to the point: "I am still alive. Please help me to get out of here...."

It was far easier than I imagined to get into Rwanda; all we had to do was show our passports and explain our situation. We spent that first night at a border town teeming with refugees. I saw sights in the camp that tore at my soul....

At a gas station [in Kigali], I found a friend of my family who knew where to find Caritas. I could hardly believe it—in a large city, I had stumbled across the one person who could help me! The friend drove us to his home and sent one of his children to fetch my sister. A few minutes later, Caritas came running in.

We hugged, cried and laughed joyously for the longest time. Caritas kept saying, "I cannot believe you have come from America to this hell to find me. You have to be my sister to do that!"

> —*Rangira Bea Gallimore, who journeyed to war-torn Rwanda to rescue her younger sister Caritas*

Tuesday morning, 18 May 1813
Before breakfast—up at half past 7

My own dear Fannikin,

   This morning and many a morning since I came to London have I blessed you for going without your breakfast for me seven years ago [to help her pack] with so much good humor as you did. You cured me completely of lying bed till *the last moment* and now I have the advantage of it every day of my life . . .

>   —*Irish novelist Maria Edgeworth writing to her sister Fanny, to whom she had signed an earlier letter: "Ever affectionately your friend—and* sister. *That last, Nature made you. The first you have made yourself and I thank you for it; and think it will add to your happiness as well as to mine. . . ."*

I sleep in the room looking out on the garden, the same that we had when we were here together six years ago. Dear Annie, you cannot think how everything here puts me in mind of you and of the time when we were here together. All the walks here and the garden, and above all our room, where you used to read to me sometimes when we had taken refuge here from the numerous troublesome children. . . .

There is more in parting than we thought when we used to talk so quietly about it. I only then thought of the actual loss of your company (you will say I valued it little enough when we were together!) and I forgot the terrible feeling of regret with which one looks back to almost every incident of our lives, regret that it is all past and sorrow at the countless things I was wrong in; things seem so pleasant when we look back at them.

> —*Rachel Henning writing to her sister Annie, who had emigrated to Australia from their home in England*

[A] romantic folk-tale tells how four young orphan sisters agreed to fill the five lancets in the north transept of York Cathedral with memorial glass, in patterns taken from their embroidery frames, which they had long laid aside for sorrow, in remembrance of a dead sister. The story further adds that they are reported to have knelt and prayed until, one by one, they passed away, and were laid to rest in a common grave. Hence these five lancets have been popularly designated the "Five Sisters."

—*from* Folk-Lore of Women *by T. F. Thiselton-Dyer*

My two sisters have been my safety nets, my life jackets, and the sources of so many discoveries and joys in my life. Now with my mother gone, it's all making sense: We are the embodiment of her, and now we need and love each other more than ever in our mother's absence.

The best thing about being a sister is the permission to be intimate—in short: *anything* goes. I have arrived at their doorsteps in complete need at various junctures of my life, and they have *always*, unconditionally been there for me. Or if there was a tangle to work through, I've learned by chipping away at it with them that there is this often painful but glorious process that guarantees closeness and enduring love.

I feel there is a perfect balance in what each of my sisters has given me. One is the comfy humorist who has allowed me to keep light; the other is the superwoman who has shown me fortitude and persistence. In both, the quality of generosity, not only in time and materials, but more in spirit, has abounded, and for this I am so grateful.

Now that I am a mother of a toddler, late in life, I thank them for the children they each have raised and whom I've been able to observe over these past twenty-two years. How they dealt with parenting and how they now participate in my son's development, lending their own invaluable experiences, is the most significant gift I could receive at this time.

Though neither sister went into music professionally, I feel they "taste" the rigors of the field I am in, always understanding and always listening—not only literally to my playing but to the vast and complex range of frustrations and elations that go hand in hand with being a performer.

With my sisters, all is forgiven, and all is given back—love, warmth, and caring in a unique bond forever.

> —*Carol Wincenc, concert flutist and Naumburg Award winner, on her sisters Jana and Linda*

We were born 10 minutes apart, Adrian first. She always said she was the real baby, and I was a kind of backup.

—Adair Lara, on her sister Adrian

LADY UTTERWORD: Hesione: are you going to kiss me or are you not?

MRS HUSHABYE: What do you want to be kissed for?

LADY UTTERWORD: I don't want to be kissed; but I do want you to behave properly and decently. We are sisters. We have been separated for twenty-three years. You ought to kiss me.

MRS HUSHABYE: Tomorrow morning dear, before you make up. I hate the smell of powder.

LADY UTTERWORD: Oh! You unfeeling—

—from George Bernard Shaw's Heartbreak House

My sister Geordie was with me in *Xochitl*, one of the six girls who danced with the fans. We traveled the country together on tour. At one stop, the conductor tried to put us off the train. He had called the police, sure that we were gypsies because of our clothes, jewelry, and our dark looks.

"No," I said to the officer who came aboard, "I will not leave the train and neither will my sister. We are not gypsies."

"We are the daughters of Dr. George Graham," Geordie said.

After a time we were believed and permitted to remain aboard the train, stay with the tour. The conductor apologized, but the drama of it all sustained us for months.

A now defunct dance magazine of the 1920s ran a cover story claiming that Geordie and I were not direct descendants of Miles Standish, but Romanian immigrants. Geordie and I arrived at their office like bats out of hell. Even though my strongest words were, and still are, "damnation" and "blue blazes," I gave them what for. Geordie exited with a particularly savory Irish insult, "I spit on you." It was always one of her favorites.

—*Martha Graham writing about her sister Geordie*

Whenever we went on walks we'd sit in the long grass on the side of the hills and Sylvia would start off on these beautiful stories. One day she found a lovely stone shining in the sun—"Norma, suppose we picked up one of these stones and there was a beautiful shiny door—and we'd open the door and go in—and on the shelves inside we'd find lots and lots of money—piles of half-crowns and florins and shillings and sixpences and threepences and pennies and halfpennies—and every time we picked up a half-crown, another one would take its place. . . ." These stories would go on and on. I was enthralled.

—Norma Warner reminiscing about her sister, educator and writer Sylvia Ashton-Warner

One of the things that has contributed to our survival has been a strong family background. I think the fact that we are family has helped us to stay together, to deal and cope with one another's problems. When one of us gets a little weak, there are others around who can strengthen her.

—Debbie Sledge, talking about her sisters Kim, Kathy, and Joni; together the four were also known as the singing group Sister Sledge

If you see someone with a funny hat, you must *not* point at it and laugh, and you must *not* be in too much of a hurry to get through the crowds to the tea table.

> —*Sisterly advice given to Princess Margaret at a garden party by her sister Princess Elizabeth (later Queen Elizabeth II)*

KATIE: We never had our own rooms our whole lives.

MEG: When I first got into the company, Katie never missed one performance.

KATIE: I was there every night. It didn't matter if it was *Firebird* monsters.

MEG: I was a monster in *Firebird* and she picked me out—

KATIE: I could tell which one she was—

MEG: —by the feet.

> —*Margaret and Kathleen Tracey, principal dancer and soloist, New York City Ballet, recalling their early days in New York together*

But let's face it, we are getting old. A nice young woman offered me her seat in a train the other day. I said, "How nice of you. I don't see why I should take your seat, but I agree that I'm much older than you, so thank you very much", and she smiled sweetly and I took it. This seems the friendlier course, I think, even when one isn't tired. . . .

On Friday we will talk about your holiday. Dear me, what should I do without these Fridays, or Saturdays, or whenever the weekly meeting is. How very lucky it is that you are so near; you might be at the other end of England, or in South Africa or somewhere, and then what *should* I do? As it is, provided you live as long as I do, or even longer, it is all right.

—Rose Macaulay, British novelist, in a 1956 letter to her sister Jean

Her presence makes the room warm and alive for me. I want to be where she is. It is not a very conscious feeling—just a vague discontent with the places where she is not. There is more life where she is. I get up and follow her when she moves from one room to another as one might unconsciously follow a moving patch of sunlight in a room.

—Anne Morrow (Lindbergh) writing about her sister Elizabeth, March 18, 1928

Back in 1979, when I was making my first tentative inroads into the music business, my sister Alice gave me—of all things—a toilet seat cover. On it were monogrammed the words, "The Twinkle." She promised that if I ever made it big, she'd give me another one labeled "The Star." But she hasn't yet.

That's my reminder that I haven't yet reached the top, that there's still so much for me to strive for and achieve. Alice's gift— or lack of one, I guess you could say—shows me that, at nearly forty, I have so much more to work for in life, so much more to look forward to.

I sure can't think of any better gift than that!

—Reba McEntire on her older sister Alice

My sister and I were alone, now, for weeks at a time, but I don't recall that we were lonely. . . . We were living safely in the unreal world of childhood. My mother always had encouraged us to cook little messes or this or that for make-believe tea parties to which we were permitted to ask our neighborhood playmates. We loved to dress up. This was called "playing grownup." We would don our mother's long skirts, pinned tight around our hips, top this by a discarded waist, all revers and braid and high collar; skewer with long hatpins a two-story hat of that day; ferret out a sunshade and gloves if possible; and in this regalia go flouncing down the street, walking with a mincing gait, speaking in an affected tone, discussing our children, our hired girls, our cookery, our clothes, our husbands in unconscious and deadly imitation of our elders.

> —*Edna Ferber, novelist and playwright, on life with her sister Fannie*

Tia and I are best friends. It's great to have your sister working on the same set. We help each other with our lines, and we give each other pointers. I can say, "Okay, Tia, you can make this funnier if you do this."

> —*Tamera Mowry, who stars with her twin sister Tia on the television series* Sister, Sister

Having my sisters in the business has given me the security to take risks in my career, because I know there will always be a hometown audience out there. That's what my sisters are to me—a guaranteed audience of two. I know I can always count on them for an honest opinion—and they laugh at the right places.

—Garry Marshall, director, writing about his sisters, actor-director Penny Marshall and producer Ronny Marshall

There was always room for one more in our big household. When the other children returned from the home of our neighbor Mrs. Brown, where they had been sent the night before because of my impending birth, they were greatly interested in viewing the new addition to the family. My ten-year-old-sister Elizabeth, feeling that some permanent record should be kept about so important an event, got her pencil, went out to the kitchen, which was in an ell of the house at the back, climbed the stairs to the "cook's room" over it, and wrote on the wall an impressive, dated announcement of my arrival!

—Ruth Painter Randall, Lincoln biographer, recounting how her sister Elizabeth welcomed her to the family

I passed three hours yesterday with my two dear sisters. All hearts opened to each other's griefs. Our sorrows and our comforts all passed in review before us from their early childhood on. Oh what a heartfelt satisfaction to hear them say as they both held me in their arms that the precepts I had early instilled in them had been of such use to them and been the comfort and support of their lives, that they owed more to me than any other human being. . . . I found both these dear hearts in perfect unison with my own.

—*Emily Lennox, Duchess of Leinster, on her sisters Sarah and Louisa, who consoled her after the death of her husband*

From our earliest moments . . . we *wanted nothing but each other* . . . She was the soul of my soul—& tis wonderful to me . . . that the first shock did not join them immediately by the flight of mine— but that over—that dreadful—harrowing—never to be forgotten moment of horrour that made me wish to be mad—over-the ties that after that first endearing period have shared with her my Heart come to my aid—Yet I was long incredulous—& still sometimes I think it is not—& that she will come.

—*Fanny Burney, 18th-century novelist, grieving over the death of her beloved sister, her "twin self"*

I would have gone through hell and high water for my sister, but at the same time, in spite of my warmest attachment to her, in the depths of my soul could be found the slightest bit of envy—that special kind of envy which we almost unconsciously cherish toward people very close to us—those whom we admire very much and would like to emulate in everything.

—*Sofia Kovalevskaia, Russian mathematician, writing about her sister Aniuta*

Although I see my three sisters less often than I do my chosen friends, and in many ways I have less in common with them, I know that if anything happened to them, I would feel as if I had lost a limb.

—*Annie Gottlieb, journalist, on her sisters*

Like all children, Marie-Rose was fascinated by fire. It was our job to keep it going and she wanted to get close to the flames just like us and move the logs around over the embers. This was strictly outside her domain, and every time she went too close to the fire, we would say: "Careful, Marie-Rose, you can get burned, don't go near it," and she'd listen. One evening, however, she got so close that her dress caught fire and burst into flames. My older sister was there, saw what happened, reacted correctly, went to grab a blanket, and got back in time to roll it around the child and save her, but both of them were burned on hands and legs; the burns were not deep but still they had to be taken care of. Sending for the doctor was out of the question. Why do that? For burns we had a remedy far more effective than any medication a pharmacist or doctor could prescribe: the potato. You cut potatoes and applied the slices to the burned areas. My sisters screamed with all their might, but they were more scared than hurt.

> —*Emilie Carles, French feminist and writer, on early life with her sisters*

My mother was a remarkable woman and quite a liberated one for her time. She was puritanically strict as to her daughters' behavior with the other sex, but she had a delicious sense of humor and was very popular with Virginia's and my peers. Our home always was a gathering place for our friends and I shudder now to think how much expense our constant informal entertaining when we lived in St. Louis must have been to our parents. We held open house every Sunday afternoon, just as Mother and her sisters had done in Nashville a generation earlier, and we felt free to invite up to a dozen or more to stay for supper.

From the time we were about ten and eleven Virginia and I always cooked dinners on Thursday nights and very proud we were of the popovers, pies, cornbread, etc. we would make. Father was so enthusiastic about our prowess as cooks that he often would suggest (jokingly, I am sure but we took him seriously) to Mother that we do all the cooking and housekeeping. We were appalled at the idea, especially at the thought of having to clean the house more than once a week. Mother believed every girl should know how to cook and clean and sew, so Virginia and I had to spend every Saturday morning helping the second maid clean the house. Before the days of vacuum cleaners, we soaked newspapers in buckets of water, then scattered the wet paper, torn into small pieces, over the carpets and swept paper and dust up together.

> —*India Edwards, journalist and Truman-era politician, recalling early life with her sister Virginia*

Sometimes I think I know everything there is to know about my sisters but this isn't true. I talk about them too much to strangers and worry afterwards that I've left out everything that is important.

Like the shadows on a sister's neck from an earring. Moving as she laughs. Look! I want to say. I have always wanted people to see everything that is beautiful about them. For the ordinary to be transformed.

—*Gillian Mears, Australian writer, on her sisters Karin, Yvonne, and Sonya*

My sister Betty, one of the most beautiful women at NYU, was my mentor, pulling me through science and math. Betty loved science; I found it incomprehensible. Betty loved new shoes; I hated them. So she broke my shoes in until they were stretched and comfortable. We cleaned each other's desks, knowing we could never throw out our own paper and notes.

—*Ruth Gruber, foreign correspondent, writing about her sister Betty*

We don't especially look alike. But our spirit is identical . . . and spirit is the essence of looks.

—*Lauren Hutton describing her younger half sister, model Kris Hall, in a 1976 interview*

I've always felt that since I was the oldest, I was the protector, the one to set the example, and the one who tried to be sure that everybody was all right, that things were under control. I still feel exactly the same way. I feel basically very motherly toward my sisters. That hasn't changed at all. If I thought they were doing something drastically wrong with their lives, I would advise them about it.

—*Joanna Simon, opera singer, recalling her role as older sister to Lucy and Carly*

If I'm not in my own home, the place I feel most comfortable is at my sister's. I was eleven years old when she was married, and I stayed up almost all night before the wedding finishing a tablecloth I hand-embroidered for her. And embroidery was never one of my strong points! I remember crying and feeling very sad when she left on her honeymoon: somehow, I was losing a rock in my life—my big sister. But that very night I moved into her very grownup just-vacated bedroom.

She brags to her friends about me, her sister "the Assembly-woman." I brag about her, too, because she is very talented and creative in her work.

We once thought about buying a house together with our husbands, and when the real estate agent asked how we would feel about sharing a kitchen, we informed her that we would be perfectly happy if the house had *no* kitchen. However, Frances does like to iron, and still hangs her laundry outside—even in her fancy patio. I put everything into the dryer.

The age difference between us disappeared when we became adults. We share the same history, so it is sometimes easy to understand each other without a lot of spoken words. She is my friend, my colleague, my sister—and I love her dearly.

> —*Loretta Weinberg, Assemblywoman for New Jersey District 37,*
> *writing about her sister, columnist and National Public Radio host*
> *Frances Halpern*

I am ten years older than my sister Loretta. By the time she was three and I was thirteen our roles in life were already evident. Whenever our mother was told how lucky she was to have a built-in baby-sitter, she'd answer, "Yes, Loretta takes very good care of Frances." Three-year-old Loretta already had the organizational skills and common-sense which her absent-minded older sister lacked.

Unrelated images rush through my mind when I think of my kid sister: a vision in smeared lipstick, clopping around in my high heels; her tears the night before my wedding when she was feeling deserted; the summer she stayed with us as a teenager and threatened to drown herself over a soured romance; the scare she gave us when, while traveling in Europe, she rushed to the Hungarian border to help victims of the failed revolution; my amazement when she needed a suit for a special event, left the car motor running, ran into the store, and came out minutes later with the outfit; the way we wept when I showed up unexpectedly for her 50th birthday bash.

My sister is decisive and surefooted. I see too many possibilities. She pushes me to make decisions. I call her "the enforcer," lovingly. Since I married at age 20, we've lived three thousand miles apart, yet we always make time to be with each other on special occasions. When she ran for political office, I flew east to walk precincts, where the strangers I met spoke of her dedication and savvy.

Her courage in the face of tough campaigns, her integrity, her smarts, all laced with a large dose of humor and a willingness to be there for family are the qualities which fill me with pride and joy in such a sister.

> —*Frances Halpern, author, columnist, and National Public Radio host, describing her younger sister Loretta Weinberg, New Jersey Assemblywoman*

My sister! My sweet sister! If a name
Dearer and purer were, it should be thine.

—*Lord Byron*, Epistle to Augusta

Round about the age of sixteen, my sister shed her chrysalis cocoon, and turned into a remarkably attractive young creature with hair like ripe corn, and a beautifully proportioned athletic figure. So far her studies had played but a small part in her life. We had both attended Miss Woolf's classes in South Audley Street at different periods of our lives. Fully realizing that the ability was there, should she choose to exert it, Miss Woolf remarked one day in a tone of idle speculation: "Isn't it interesting how two members of the same family can be so different? Your sister, of course won *all* the prizes."

The result was electrifying. Galvanized, on her mettle, Sonia managed to atone in six months for the inattention of several years. Practically every talent was hers to develop; she was musical, possessed a lovely mezzo-soprano voice, danced like a dream, wrote with facility and verve, the only gift she did not possess—I think she would be the first to admit this—was the gift of drawing; and even that is not strictly true. She could produce very small, meticulous, painfully literal renderings of mostly utilitarian objects. Flights of fancy were not for her.

> —*Violet Trefusis, Victorian memoirist known for her affair with Vita Sackville-West, writing about her younger sister Sonia*

At fifteen I admired and envied my sister Dot, who would never shrink from scenes. When she felt like it, she threw things. Even when she threw them at me, I admired her swift passion as well as her aim.

—Emily Hahn, journalist, writing about her sister Dorothy

Truly, there is no friend like a sister. I can give testimony to that. My sister is like a security blanket to me. I always know that she is there, and that I can depend on her. She has been and is always supportive of everything that I do. My sister is largely responsible for my having achieved so much in my life; I don't think I could have done any of it without my sister. Her name is Marion Taylor Hummons and I love her.

—Dr. Margaret T. A. Burroughs, retired teacher and founder of the DuSable Museum, writing about her sister Marion, retired Chicago postal secretary and volunteer at Chicago's DuSable Museum of African-American History

As I sit and look on these mountains, so grand and flowing and the illimitable aerial blue, beyond and over, I seem to realize with peculiar force that bountiful, fathomless heart of Elizabeth, forever disappointed, but forever believing; sorely rebuffed yet never bitter; robbed day by day, yet giving again, from endless store; more sweet, more tender, more serene, as the hours pass over her, though they may drop gall instead of flowers upon this unguarded heart.

> —*Sophia Peabody Hawthorne, painter and wife of Nathaniel Hawthorne, describing her sister Elizabeth's complex emotions, in a letter to their mother, September 29, 1850*

She is a beautiful girl . . . I think she will write *something great one of these days.* . . . I think perhaps one reason why other girls are not more attractive may be because I have been so much with Louisa who is so uncommonly interesting & funny that beside her, other girls seem commonplace.

—*Anna Alcott describing her sister, novelist Louisa May Alcott*

She [Abbie] is so graceful and pretty and loves beauty so much, it is hard for her to be poor and wear other people's ugly things. You and I have learned not to mind *much*, but when I think of her, I long to dash out and buy the finest hat the limited sum of ten dollars can procure. . . . I hope I shall live long enough to see the dear child in silk and lace, with plenty of pictures and bottles of cream, Europe, and all she longs for.

—*Louisa May Alcott confiding in her sister Anna about their sister Abbie, who is clearly the model for Amy in* Little Women

To C.M. on Her Prison Birthday

February, 1917

What has time to do with thee,
Who hast found the victors' way
To be rich in poverty,
Without sunshine to be gay,
To be free in a prison cell?
Nay, on that undreamed judgment day,
When, on the old world's scrap-heap flung,
Powers and empires pass away,
Radiant and unconquerable
Thou shalt be young.

> —*Eva Gore-Booth's poem for her sister, Irish rebel heroine Constance, Countess Markievicz*

There was no one ever like her. She was something wonderful and beautiful, and so simple and thought so little of herself. I don't think she ever knew how much she was to me. . . .

But her gentleness prevented me from getting very brutal, and one does get very callous in a War. I once held out and stopped a man being shot because of her. And she was always there when I was down and out. . . .

I'm not coming over [to her funeral] because I simply could not face it all. I want to keep my last memory of her so happy and peaceful, and nothing but love and beauty and peace.

> —*Constance Gore-Booth, Countess Markievicz, Irish rebel and an organizer of the Easter Rising, writing to a friend on the death of her sister and tireless supporter, poet Eva Gore-Booth*

ELSIE: When we rode, we'd leave right after breakfast and ride all day. It took us most of the day to locate all our horses and cattle; some of them would stray eight or ten miles. When the roundup wagon came through, we'd ride down while they were working the herds and make sure all our cattle were cut out and left. That's how we learned about cattle and the roundups, by doing it for ourselves and the neighbors. And then after we became acquainted with the roundup men, we started to ride circle with them and help work the herds just like the rest of the men.

We were the only girls that ever rode with the roundup. I don't know why, unless it's due to the fact that Dad sent us out to take care of our own stock and we got started doing it and nobody else did. There weren't many girls in the country who rode to the extent we did.

AMY: This wagon boss—we always called him Father Tug—came around in the spring. Elsie and I were shucking grain. He said, "Cooksley, I need your girls." Dad said, "Well, you can't have them. I need them too. They are shucking grain."

"I need them worse than you do," said Father Tug. "I've got a bunch of kids out of Sheridan that don't know one end of a cow from the other, and I've got beef roundup to work. I'll make you a deal. I'll send two of those boys over here to shuck grain if you'll let me have your girls to go with the wagon."

So that pleased us! We'd lots rather ride a horse than shuck grain.

—*Elsie Lloyd and Amy Chubb, cowgirls and sisters, recalling their early years*

The only time Diana and I were peaceful, when I wasn't shrieking "She did it, she did it!" or "Not fair!" was in bed, in the dark, when I changed her name to Jane and mine to Marie and we conversed. Of what I can scarcely imagine. But I suppose I said things like, "Would you like more ice cream, Jane?" and she answered, "That would be very nice, Marie."

Other times I tapped out tunes on the maple headboard of my bed. "Baa, baa, black sheep!" Diana would guess, and "Lazy Mary, will you get up!" I liked her then. Even more I liked not being alone in the dark. I liked the sound of her breathing—she was always asleep before I was—and the companionable creak of the mattress when she tossed and turned.

> —*Mary Cantwell, journalist and essayist, writing about her sister*
> *Diana*

This sister, though only just entering her teens, was toughening herself by all sorts of unnecessary hardships for whatever might await her womanhood. She used frequently to sleep in the garret on a hard wooden chest instead of in a bed. And she would get up before daylight and run over into the burying-ground, barefooted and white-robed (we lived for two or three years in another house than our own, where the oldest graveyard in town was only separated from us by our garden fence), "to see if there were any ghosts there," she told us. Returning noiselessly, a smiling phantom, with long, golden-brown hair rippling over her shoulders,—she would drop a trophy upon her little sisters' pillow, in the shape of a big, yellow apple that had dropped from "the Colonel's" "pumpkin sweeting" tree into the graveyard, close to our fence.

She was fond of giving me surprises, of watching my wonder at seeing anything beautiful for the first time. Once, when I was very little, she made me supremely happy by rousing me before four o'clock in the morning, dressing me hurriedly, and taking me out with her for a walk across the graveyard and through the dewy fields. The birds were singing, and the sun was just rising, and we were walking toward the east, hand in hand. . . .

—*Lucy Larcom, abolitionist and poet, on her oldest sister Emilie*

My mind is not in the most cheerful state. Trials of various kinds seem to be reserved for our gray Hairs, for our declining years. Shall I receive good and not evil? I will not forget the blessings which sweeten Life. One of those is the prospect I have before me of meeting my dear sister soon, I hope in health and spirits. A strong imagination is said to be a refuge from sorrow, and a kindly solace for a feeling Heart.

> *—Abigail Adams in a letter to her sister Mary Smith Cranch, dated May 26, 1800*

Emily is nineteen. She's in law school. She got married at fifteen. . . . She's a unique person, all right. I don't think that she likes me very much. I think she thinks I have too many problems when life, according to her, has been so simple. I am sure she feels herself, secretly, to be the older sister. I have never known her to be a real child.

> *—from* The Odd Woman *by Gail Godwin*

Although she's younger, thinner, cuter, and married to the perfect man, she has managed to maintain the perfect balance between confident indignance and insecure, guilt-ridden paranoia that I have strived for all my life.

—*Cathy Guisewite, cartoonist, on her sister Mickey*

We are not *only* sisters. It is an amazing and sort of doubly strong association to be linked instinctively (and by environment, early life, etc.) *and* by one's desire and reason. It is a rare relationship. I feel as though you have leaned down and lifted me up to where you were so many times. At least if we have had things together your having them first or at the same time has helped me to realize and comprehend better what was happening. Having an experience with someone else enriches it *so* much. You feel for them and yourself.

—*Anne Morrow (Lindbergh) in a letter to her sister, Elizabeth, March 1928*

Mom and Daddy married late in life and had three daughters in the next seven years. We came from a working-class family where loyalty to your family, your faith, and your work was paramount. I can still recall my father teaching my sisters and me to always do at least a day and a half's work for a day's pay. And we all remember with pride the beauty and inspiration in the poems composed and shared aloud with us by our mother.

My parents' talents were passed on to their daughters, and we use them daily in the work we do together. My sister Regina helps me edit my books and checks my spelling, a gift she inherited from our father, and one I don't share. My sister Mary fills in for my husband and me on our local talk radio show when we're out of town, and sings the opening theme song for us. Her voice is a wonderful reminder of how our mother sang to us as children.

How proud Mom and Daddy must be of their daughters as they look down from Heaven and see how we three sisters have preserved their memories in our work, our faith, and our commitment to staying close as a family.

—*JoAnna M. Lund, author and entrepreneur, on her sisters Regina and Mary*

I think that I had an attachment for my eldest sister and that she was very fond and proud of me. I remember that between ten and twelve I felt unhappy before going to sleep and Emilie was kind enough to move her couch near to mine and I went to sleep holding her hand.

—*Melanie Klein, psychoanalyst, on her sister Emilie*

My sister Georgina was born the day after my own birthday, when I was nine. I always felt as if she was my own child. I could immediately cuddle her, and I could dress her up as well. Dolls weren't my cup of tea—I always had teddy bears—but she was my doll and I absolutely adored her. I was an only child until I got my sister, and I was lonely. I didn't know anybody who was just by themselves. Everybody always had brothers and sisters, and I didn't.

When my sister was born, I was called to the headmistress's study at Tring. Of course I was petrified as I was such a naughty child I was often called there, and I thought, "Oh, God, what have I done now?" And she said, "I've got some very good news for you. Your father's on the phone"—you see, he was waiting to speak to me. And he said, "You've got the most wonderful baby sister."

—*Antoinette Sibley, ballerina, writing about her little sister Georgina*

My twin, Paola...had shown from early infancy a great artistic talent which aroused in me unconditional admiration, unsullied by envy or regret, because I was completely lacking in her gift. This was only one of the differences between us evident from the first years of our lives. The others, no less significant, and which revealed at first glance our non-identical twinship, were manifest in our physical appearance, in our characters, and in our behavior. Her face differed from my own in shape and in its every feature. Beneath a high, slightly convex forehead, her laughing blue eyes denoted a disposition (in truth, more apparent than real) to a gaiety that enchanted our father. From an early age...her face bore an extraordinary resemblance to his own—a cause for joy and paternal pride. On the other hand, our mother was pleased to assert that I was the living image of her mother...whom she had adored and lost in adolescence. The deep affection linking Paola to our father, reciprocated with the most heartfelt tenderness, and that between myself and my mother date back to that early time. As for the relationship between Paola and myself, from our earliest childhood up to today—a period spanning over three quarters of a century— it has been characterized by an intensity of affection so great as to have created, especially while we were children, a sort of barrier against the intrusion of third parties.

—*Rita Levi-Montalcini, Nobel Prize winner for Medicine, 1986, writing about her sister Paola*

Our story of sisterhood is different, as you will soon see,
We were born of one egg—two wombmates, never only me.
Our special closeness began at birth—ground zero
And our bond has strengthened my life; she's my #1 hero.
Do we fight? Do we argue? Do we disagree?
But of course—we're sisters *and* best friends, that's the key.
Most spend their lives searching day after day
For that one special someone who'll wash their sorrows away,
With my sis at my side, there's no problem too tough,
No matter how trying, it's never too rough.

We've been through a lot, my sister and I,
When we lost our father, on her shoulder I'd cry,
But having a friend to share in my pain
Helped in the healing and my life to regain.
She's my partner in business, hard-working and fair,
She's my soulmate and likeness, from toes to long red hair,
My best friend, my sister, my comfort when I'm alone,
A buddy to sleep with when night monsters roam.
A sister you can't lie to about how much you weigh,
A constant encouragement day after day.
We've been separated once, to distant ends of the land,
But our bond is inseparable like the sea and the sand.

Ever since we were small, we dreamed of owning our own restaurant—and now do: Twins, our New York restaurant where all the staff are twins—soulmates times two. We've got a third sister, Lisi, which makes us a pair with a spare. She's the third leg of our sisterly triangle, and we treasure our friendship.

> —Lisa Ganz, *co-owner of the restaurant* Twins *with her sister*
> *Debbie, on her two sisters*

Oh my dearest Pop,

I wish I could tell you how I love you & thank you for your kind thoughts as received in your letter today. If you did but know how genial it is to me, when my dear people give me a hope of their blessing & that they would speed me on my way—as the kind thought of Cromford [near her grandmother's home] seems to say they are ready to do. I will write to Mama about Paris & Cromford.

My Pop, whether at one or the other, my heart will be with thee. Now, if these seem mere words, because bodily I shall be leaving you, have patience with me, my dearest. I hope that you & I shall live to prove a true love to each other.

I cannot, during the year's rounds, go the way which (for my sake, I know) you have wished. There have been times when, for your dear sake, I have tried to stifle the thoughts which I feel ingrained in my nature. But, if that may not be, I hope that something better shall be. If I ask your blessing on a part of my time for my absence, I hope to be all the happier.

> —*Florence Nightingale's letter to her sister Parthenope, as she left home to nurse in Paris*

My dear Mary—

. . . You begin by saying that no one who would love you as you want to be loved—would find what they want in you.—Now I should like to know *how you wanted to be loved* & wherein my love of you has failed—if it has failed—You say you have not satisfied my intellect when you have satisfied my moral sense—I will reply that you have always satisfied my intellect—when you have done justice to your own—& never disappointed me in that way except when you have stopped short—through some whim—on a course of thought.

—*Elizabeth Peabody, educator and publisher of Emerson's literary journal* The Dial, *in a letter to her sister, Mary Peabody, later Mrs. Horace Mann, dated May 16, 1836*

My sister Mary was working in the Oakland A's office at the time, and a girl had written in suggesting that girls instead of boys be hired to police the foul lines. *Anything* new and novel appealed to Charlie Finley, one of the most free-spirited men who ever owned a baseball team, and he bought the idea. "Why not try for it?" Mary suggested to me. "Go on in and see if you can get the job." The minute I heard about it, I knew, absolutely *knew*; that job belonged to me and nobody else. I borrowed my sister's best outfit and my mom drove me to the team's office, where I was interviewed by the secretaries. By the time I reached the office, I was absolutely glowing with anticipation. The interviewing secretaries never had a choice—the way I presented myself, destiny had brought me into the world for one purpose only, retrieving foul balls on the third-base line at Oakland Alameda County Stadium. I was hired, and I was in ecstasy.

> —*Debbi Fields crediting her sister Mary with helping her get her first real job*

I *have* lost a treasure, such a Sister, such a friend, as never can have been surpassed,—she was the sun of my life, the gilder of every pleasure, the soother of every sorrow, I had not a thought concealed from her, & it is as if I had lost a part of myself.

> —*Cassandra Austen writing to her favorite niece, Fanny, after the death of her sister Jane*

I was born on Webster Street in South Philadelphia in a room my parents had rented when they were married. I was about two years old when we first moved to my grandmother's. She had a big house, and there was going to be more room for the three of us and the new baby. My earliest recollection is of the third-story room my parents occupied in that house. Somehow I was in the room—I had crawled under the bed when the doctor had arrived and perhaps had fallen asleep there. I heard a cry. It was the first cry of my new sister, Alyce. I peeked out. There was the doctor and there was his black bag. Long after I should have known better, I believed that Alyce had been fetched in that black bag.

> —*Marian Anderson, African-American contralto who performed on the steps of the Lincoln Memorial, recalling the birth of her sister Alyce*

We were close as children and are still close today. But we're so different that there's never been any serious competition, no threatening rivalry. She has always done the glamorous things. She became a model. I became a photographer. She became a film star. I married one.

—*Berry Berenson talking about her sister, actress Marisa Berenson*

When I slice the end off my finger with a kitchen gadget, my sister says, "I did the exact same thing last year!"

Being an older sister, she bandaged it herself and never bothered to tell me. Being a younger sister, I called her from the emergency room at Roosevelt Hospital, where the top hand surgeon in New York was taking care of me. Thanks to birth order, my sister has something I'll never have: a need to be brave. And I have something she'll never have: a powerhouse to be inspired by.

—*Patricia Volk, journalist, writing about her sister Jo Ann*

While she was still a schoolgirl there were paragraphs in the papers, which used to annoy Father very much, saying a raving beauty was growing up in Richmond, Virginia, who would become the talk of the country. It was not then considered the thing to be talked about in the papers, and I remember when, later, one of them printed Irene's picture, Father threatened to go to New York and shoot the editor.

Irene wasn't only beautiful. She had wonderful charm . . . When she came in, it was like the sun streaming into the room. Nor did the praise and adulation she got ever go to her head. She remained entirely unspoiled and this was wonderful. Mostly she laughed at the fuss people made of her, and no doubt her brothers and sisters played their part in keeping her humble. I remember once when she came back from a visit where she had been the belle of every ball and the papers had been full of flattering paragraphs about her, saying she was the loveliest girl in America and bid fair to become a reigning belle—we all fell on her. "You may have looked beautiful at the party," we told her, "but people ought to see the way you look now."

> —*Nancy Langhorne, later Lady Astor and first female Member of Parliament, reminiscing about her sister Irene, who married Charles Dana Gibson and inspired "the Gibson girl"*

We were waked by the ticking of the bells,—the bells tick in Amherst, to tell the fireman. I sprang to the window, and each side of the curtain saw that awful sun. The moon was shining high at the time, and the birds singing like trumpets.

Vinnie came soft as a moccasin, "Don't be afraid, Emily, it is only the fourth of July."

I did not tell her that I saw it, for I thought if she felt it best to deceive, it must be that it was. . . .

I could hear buildings falling, and oil exploding, and people walking and talking gayly, and cannon soft as velvet for parishes that did not know that we were burning up.

And so much lighter than day was it, that I saw a caterpillar measure a leaf far down the orchard; and Vinnie kept saying bravely, "It's only the fourth of July". . . .

Vinnie's "only fourth of July" I shall always remember. I think she will tell us so when we die, to keep us from being afraid.

> —*Emily Dickinson writing about her sister Lavinia in a letter to friends in 1879*

Sources

Abbajay, Mary, interview

Abbajay, Stephanie, interview

Adams, Abigail, *New Letters of Abigail Adams, 1788-1801*, Greenwood Press

Alcott, Anna, *The Alcotts: Biography of a Family* by Madelon Bell, Clarkson Potter

Alcott, Louisa May, *The Alcotts: Biography of a Family* by Madelon Bell, Clarkson Potter

Alcott, Louisa May, *The Journals of Louisa May Alcott*, Little, Brown & Company and the Estate of Theresa W. Pratt

Alcott, Louisa May, *Little Women*, Frederick Warne & Company, London

Allen, Gracie, *Woman's Home Companion*, March 1953

Anderson, Loni, *My Life in High Heels*, William Morrow and Company

Anderson, Marian, *My Lord, What a Morning*, The Viking Press

Andrews, Maxene, *New Yorker*, November 11, 1991

Antigone, Sophocles, Oxford University Press

Armstrong, Karen, *Through the Narrow Gate*, St. Martin's Press

Ashley, Mary, *Edwina: Countess Mountbatten of India* by Richard A. Hough, Weidenfeld & Nicolson

Ashton-Warner, Sylvia, *I Passed This Way*, Alfred A. Knopf, Inc.

Asquith, Margot, *The Autobiography of Margot Asquith*, edited by Mark Bonham Carter, Houghton Mifflin

Astor, Nancy Langhorne, *Nancy: The Life of Lady Astor* by Christopher Sykes, Harper & Row

Atkins, Dale V., Ph.D., *Sisters*, Arbor House Publishing

Austen, Cassandra (mother), *Memoir of Jane Austen* by E. Austen-Leigh, Oxford University Press

Austen, Cassandra (sister), letter to Fanny Knight in *Jane Austen's Letters*, Oxford University Press

Austen, Jane, *Sense and Sensibility*, Penguin Books

Baez, Joan, *Daybreak*, The Dial Press, Inc.

Barber, Mary, interview

Bardot, Mijanou, *Bardot: An Intimate Portrait* by Jeffrey Robinson, Donald I. Fine Books

Barton, Clara, *The Story of My Childhood*, Baker & Taylor Company (reissued 1980 by Arno Press, Inc.)

Bell, Vanessa, *Selected Letters of Vanessa Bell*, Pantheon Books

Berenson, Berry, *Cosmopolitan*, May 1976

Berlin, Irving, "Sisters" from *White Christmas*, copyright © 1953 by Irving Berlin. Used by permission. All rights reserved.

Berry, Bertice, Ph.D., *Bertice: The World According to Me*, Scribner

Blackwell, Antoinette, *Friends and Sisters*, University of Illinois Press

Bourke-White, Margaret, *Margaret Bourke-White: A Biography* by Vicki Goldberg, Harper & Row

Brontë, Charlotte, quoted in *The Brontës* by Katherine Frank, Houghton Mifflin Company

Brooks, June, *Flashbacks*, Alfred A. Knopf, Inc.

Browning, Elizabeth Barrett, *Elizabeth Barrett's Diary*, John Murray Publishers, Ltd.

Browning, Elizabeth Barrett, *The Brownings' Correspondence*, Wedgestone Press

Burana, Lily, *Mademoiselle*, September 1995

Burney, Fanny, *Frances Burney: The Life in the Works* by Margaret Ann Doody, Rutgers University Press

Burney, Fanny, *The Famous Miss Burney* by Barbara Schrank and David J. Supino, John Day

Burney, Susanna, *Fanny Burney and Her Friends*, edited by L. B. Seeley, Seeley and Co., Ltd.

Burroughs, Dr. Margaret T. A., interview

Byron, Lord, *Epistle to Augusta*

Callaway, Ann Hampton, interview

Callaway, Liz, interview

Campbell, Mrs. Patrick, *Mrs. Pat: The Life of Mrs. Patrick Campbell* by Margot Peters, Alfred A. Knopf, Inc.

Cannon, Ophelia Colley [Minnie Pearl], *Minnie Pearl: An Autobiography*, Simon and Schuster

Cantwell, Mary, *American Girl: Scenes From a Small-Town Childhood*, Random House, Inc.

Capote, Truman, *The Grass Harp*, Random House, Inc.

Cardwell Lawson, Charity, *New York Times*, July 7, 1994

Carles, Emilie, *A Life of Her Own: A Countrywoman in Twentieth Century France*, Penguin Books

Cather, Willa, *The World of Willa Cather* by Mildred R. Bennett, University of Nebraska Press

Christie, Agatha, *An Autobiography*, Collins (London)

Collins, Jackie, *People*, November 12, 1984

Conner, Susan, interview

Conroy, Pat, *Prince of Tides*, Houghton Mifflin Company

Corpening, Sara, interview

Davis, Sonya, *Essence*, May 1983

de Beauvoir, Hélène, *Simone de Beauvoir: A Biography* by Deidre Bair, Summit Books

de Beauvoir, Simone, *Memoirs of a Dutiful Daughter*, Harper & Row

Delany, Sarah, *Having Our Say*, Kodansha America, Inc.

Devine, Loretta, interview

Dickinson, Emily, *Emily Dickinson: A Biography* by Cynthia G. Wolff, Alfred A. Knopf, Inc.

Digby Moore, Sheila [on Pamela Harriman], *Vanity Fair*, July 1988

Dillard, Annie, *An American Childhood*, Harper & Row

Dinesen, Isak, *Letters From Africa 1914-1931*, University of Chicago Press

Drabble, Margaret, *A Summer Bird-Cage*, William Morrow and Company, Inc.

Du Maurier, Daphne, *Myself When Young*, Doubleday & Company, Inc.

Edgeworth, Maria, *Letters From England, 1813-1844*, Oxford at the Clarendon Press

Edwards, India, *Pulling No Punches*, G. P. Putnam's Sons

Elizabeth, Princess, quoted in James Brough, *The Tragic Princess*, G. P. Putnam's Sons

Elizabeth, Queen, quoted in Elizabeth Longford's *The Queen*, Alfred A. Knopf, Inc.

Farrell, Suzanne, *Holding On To the Air*, Summit Books

Ferber, Edna, *A Peculiar Treasure*, Doubleday & Company, Inc.

Fields, Debbi, *One Smart Cookie*, Simon and Schuster

Frank, Anne, *Diary of Anne Frank*, Doubleday

Franks, Lucinda, *Wild Apples*, Random House, Inc.

Gallimore, Rangira Bea, *Ladies Home Journal*, February 1995

Ganz, Lisa, interview

Garbo, Greta, *Garbo: A Biography* by Barry Paris, Alfred A. Knopf, Inc.

Garner, Helen, "A Scrapbook, An Album" from *Sisters*, ed. by Drusilla Modjeska, Angus & Robertson

Gifford, Kathie Lee, *I Can't Believe I Said That!*, Pocket Books

Gilbert, Melissa, *Harpers Bazaar*, July 1994

Gish, Dorothy, *Stage* magazine c. 1917, quoted in *The Movies, Mr. Griffith and Me* by Lillian Gish with Ann Pinchot, Prentice-Hall Inc.

Gish, Lillian, *Stage* magazine c. 1917

Givens, Stephanie, *Ebony*, December 1991

Glasgow, Ellen, *The Woman Within*, Harcourt, Brace and Company

Godden, Rumer, *A House with Four Rooms*, William Morrow and Company, Inc.

Godwin, Gail, *The Odd Woman*, Alfred A. Knopf, Inc.

Gone with the Wind screenplay by Sidney Howard from the novel by Margaret Mitchell, Dell Publishing

Gore-Booth, Constance, *The Prison Letters of Countess Markievicz*, Virago Press

Gore-Booth, Eva, *The Prison Letters of Countess Markievicz*, Virago Press

Gottlieb, Annie, "The Sister Knot," *Mademoiselle*, November 1980

Graham, Martha, *Blood Memory*, Doubleday

Graves, Denyce, interview

Gruber, Ruth, *Ahead of Time: My Early Years as a Foreign Correspondent*, Wynwood Press

Guisewite, Cathy, *Dancing Through Life in a Pair of Broken Heels*, Bantam Books

Hahn, Emily, *Times and Places*, Thomas Y. Crowell Company

Haizlip, Shirlee Taylor, *The Sweeter the Juice*, Simon and Schuster

Halpern, Frances, interview

Hatta, Mari, interview

Hawthorne, Sophia Peabody, *Elizabeth Peabody, American Renaissance Woman*, Wesleyan University Press

Henner, Marilu, *Marilu*, Pocket Books

Henning, Rachel, *The Letters of Rachel Henning*, Penguin Books

Holt, Hazel, *A Lot to Ask: A Life of Barbara Pym*, Dutton

Howard, Jane, *A Different Woman*, E. P. Dutton and Company, Inc.

Hoyt, Nancy, *Elinor Wylie: Portrait of an Unknown Lady*, The Bobbs-Merrill Company

Hubert-Whitten, Janet, *Ebony*, December 1991

Hutton, Lauren, *Cosmopolitan*, May 1976

Jolley, Elizabeth, "My Sister Dancing" from *Sisters*, edited by Drusilla Modjeska, Angus & Robertson

Joplin, Laura, *Love, Janis*, Villard Books

Kelly, Lizanne, quoted in *Grace: The Secret Lives of a Princess* by James Spada, Dolphin/Doubleday

King, Nina, *Grace King: A Southern Destiny* by Robert Bush, Louisiana State University Press

Klein, Melanie, *Melanie Klein: Her World and Her Work* by Phyllis Grosskurth, Alfred A. Knopf, Inc.

Kovalevskaia, Sofia, *A Convergence of Lives* by A. H. Koblitz, Birkhauser-Boston, Inc.

LaBelle, Patti, *McCall's*, April 1994

Labeque, Katia, *Harpers Bazaar*, April 1990

Lagerlof, Selma, *Memories of My Childhood*, Doubleday, Doran and Company

Lara, Adair, *Welcome to Earth, Mom*, Chronicle Books

Larcom, Lucy, *A New England Girlhood*, Peter Smith

Larcom, Lucy, *Boston Transcript*, July 27, 1889

Lawrence, D. H., *Women in Love*, Alfred A. Knopf, Inc.

Lee, Gypsy Rose, "Mother and the Knights of Pythias," *The New Yorker*, April 10, 1943

Leimbach, Marti, *Mademoiselle*, April 1990

Lennon, Dianne, *Same Song, Separate Voices*, Roundtable Publishing, Inc.

Lennon, Janet, *Same Song, Separate Voices*, Roundtable Publishing, Inc.

Lennon, Kathy, *Same Song, Separate Voices*, Roundtable Publishing, Inc.

Lennon, Peggy, *Same Song, Separate Voices*, Roundtable Publishing, Inc.

Lennox, Emily, *Aristocrats* by Stella Tillyard, Chatto & Windus, London

Levertov, Denise, *Tesserae*, New Directions Books

Levi-Montalcini, Rita, *In Praise of Imperfection*, Basic Books

Lewis, Sarah, *Wise Men Fish Here: Frances Steloff and the Gotham Book Mart* by W. G. Rogers, Harcourt, Brace & World

Li, Amy, *Sisters on Sisters*, Grapevine, Thorsons Publishing Group

Lindbergh, Anne Morrow, *Bring Me a Unicorn*, Harcourt Brace Jovanovich

Lloyd, Elsie, and Chubb, Amy, from *Cowgirls* by Teresa Jordan, Anchor Press

Lovenheim, Barbara, *Glamour*, March 1980

Luft, Lorna, *People*, June 7, 1993

Lund, JoAnna, interview

Lynn, Loretta, *Loretta Lynn: Coal Miner's Daughter*, Bernard Geis Associates, Inc.

Macaulay, Rose, *Letters to a Sister*, Atheneum

Maleeva, Manuela, *Sports Illustrated*, December 3, 1990

Mandrell, Barbara, *Get to the Heart*, Bantam Books

Mandrell, Louise, *The Barbara Mandrell Story*, G. P. Putnam's Sons

Mansfield, Katherine, *The Collected Letters of Katherine Mansfield, vol. 1: 1903–1917*, Oxford University Press, and The Society of Authors as the literary representative of the Estate of Katharine Mansfield

Marks, Jean, interview

Marshall, Garry, *McCall's*, November 1992

Martin, Debora, interview

Martin, Mary, *My Heart Belongs*, William Morrow and Company, Inc.

Maynard, Joyce, *USA Weekend*, January 27–29, 1995

McCullers, Carson, "The Discovery of Christmas," *Mademoiselle*, December 1953

McEntire, Reba, *Reba: My Story*, Bantam Books

McGarrigle, Kate, *Rolling Stone*, March 31, 1983

McNeill, Louise, *The Milkweed Ladies*, University of Pittsburgh Press

Mead, Margaret, *Blackberry Winter*, William Morrow & Company, Inc.

Mears, Gillian, "The Childhood Gland" from *Sisters*, ed. by Drusilla Modjeska, Angus & Robertson

Mesta, Perle, *Perle: My Story*, McGraw-Hill

Millay, Edna St. Vincent, *Letters of Edna St. Vincent Millay*, Harper & Brothers

Miller, Marie-Chantal, *Vogue*, July 1995

Minnelli, Liza, *People*, June 7, 1993

Miracle, Berniece Baker, *My Sister, Marilyn: A Memoir of Marilyn Monroe*, Algonquin Books

Mitford, Jessica, *Daughters and Rebels*, The Riverside Press

Montagu, Lady Mary W., *The Lost Art: Letters of 7 Famous Women* by Van Doren, Coward-McCann, Inc.

Moulton-Barrett, Henrietta, *The Brownings' Correspondence*, Wedgestone Press

Mowry, Tamera, *Ebony*, February 1995

Myrdal, Alva, *Alva Myrdal: A Daughter's Memoir* by Sissela Bok, Addison-Wesley

Negroni, Lorie Christine, and Negroni, Andrea Lee, interview

Nightingale, Florence, *Ever Yours, Florence Nightingale: Selected Letters*, Virago Press

Nikuradse, Tamara, interview

O'Brien, Tamara, *Prism of the Night* by Katherine Ramsland, Plume Books

O'Keefe, Kathleen, interview

Parton, Dolly, *Dolly: My Life and Other Unfinished Business*, HarperCollins Publishers, Inc.

Peabody, Elizabeth, *Letters of Elizabeth Peabody, American Renaissance Woman*, Wesleyan University Press

Pemberton, Gayle, "None of the Above," *The Yale Review*, July 1990

Pontillon, Edma, *Berthe Morisot: The Correspondence with Her Family and Friends*, Camden Press, Ltd.

Porter, Katherine Anne, *Letters of Katherine Anne Porter*, The Atlantic Monthly Press

Potter, Maggie, *Beatrice Webb* by Kitty Muggeridge and Ruth Adam, Alfred A. Knopf, Inc.

Pym, Barbara, *Some Tame Gazelle*, E. P. Dutton, Inc.

Radziwill, Lee Bouvier, *One Special Summer*, Delacorte Press

Rambert, Dame Marie, *Quicksilver*, Macmillan London Limited

Randall, Ruth Painter, *I Ruth: Autobiography of a Marriage*, Little, Brown and Company

Rashad, Phylicia, *McCall's*, July 1987

Reddy, Helen, *Mademoiselle*, October 1977

Redgrave, Lynn, *Mademoiselle*, October 1977

Redgrave, Vanessa, *Vanessa Redgrave: An Autobiography*, Random House, Inc.

Rice, Anne, *Prism of the Night* by Katherine Ramsland, Plume Books

Ritchie, Anne T., *Anne Thackeray Ritchie: A Biography* by Winifred Gerin, Oxford University Press

Rossetti, Christina, "Goblin Market" from *The Poetical Works of Christina Rossetti*, Little, Brown and Company

Sanger, Margaret, *Margaret Sanger: An Autobiography*, W. W. Norton & Company

Schlesinger, Marian Cannon, *Snatched from Oblivion*, Little, Brown and Company

Scott, Bess Whitehead, *You Meet Such Interesting People*, Texas A&M University Press

Sharpnack, Sharon, interview

Shaw, George Bernard, *Heartbreak House*, Brentano's (1919)

Shriver, Eunice Kennedy, *Saturday Evening Post*, September 1962

Sibley, Antoinette, *Antoinette Sibley; Reflections of a Ballerina* by Barbara Newman, Hutchinson

Simon, Joanna, quoted in *Sisters* by Elizabeth Fishel, Conari Press

Sledge, Debbie, *Mademoiselle*, June 1981

Smith, Margarita G., *The Mortgaged Heart*, Houghton Mifflin Company

Smith, Sally Bedell, *In All His Glory: The Life of William S. Paley*, Simon and Schuster

Stahl, Zoe, interview

Talbo, Dolly, *The Grass Harp* by Truman Capote, Random House, Inc.

Tan, Amy, *The Joy Luck Club*, G. P. Putnam's Sons

Thackeray, Minny, *Anne Thackeray Ritchie: A Biography* by Winifred Gerin, Oxford University Press

Thiselton-Dyer, T. F., *Folk-Lore of Women*, A. C. McClurg & Co.

Tolstoy, Sonya, *Sonya: The Life of Countess Tolstoy* by Anne Edwards, Simon and Schuster

Tracey, Margaret and Kathleen, *New Dance Review*, March–April 1989

Trefusis, Violet, *Don't Look Round: Reminiscences*, Viking Penguin

Turner, Cali Rae, interview

Van Buren, Abigail, quoted in *Dear Abby, Dear Ann* by Janice Pottker, Dodd, Mead & Company

Volk, Patricia, *Redbook*, August 1995

von Richthofen, Frieda, *Frieda Lawrence: The Memoirs and Correspondence*, Alfred A. Knopf, Inc.

Vonnegut, Kurt, *Welcome to the Monkey House*, Delacorte Press

Warner, Norma, *Sylvia!*, Viking Penguin

Weinberg, Loretta, interview

West, Dame Rebecca, *Family Memories*, Viking Penguin

Wharton, Edith, "The Bunner Sisters" from *Xingu*, Charles Scribner's Sons

Whitney, Gertrude V., *Gertrude Vanderbilt Whitney* by B. H. Friedman, Doubleday & Company, Inc.

Wilder, Laura Ingalls, *Laura: The Life of Laura Ingalls Wilder* by Donald Zochert, Henry Regnery

Wiley, Bennie, *Ebony*, December 1991

Wincenc, Carol, interview

Winkler-Kaplan, Barbara, interview

Wood, Lana, *Natalie: A Memoir by her Sister*, G. P. Putnam's Sons

Wood, Monica, *Secret Language*, Faber & Faber, Inc.

Woolf, Virginia, *Letters of Virginia Woolf*, Hogarth Press

Yahp, Beth, "Houses, Sisters, Cities" in *Sisters*, ed. by Drusilla
    Modjeska, Angus & Robertson
Young, Gene, interview
Zanger, Sally R., interview

Author's Note

I want to express my appreciation to Meg Ruley, my agent and longtime friend, who responded to this project with such enthusiasm, and to Denise Silvestro, my editor, for sharing my fascination with the subject of sisterly friendship. Their warmth and dedication are unmatched. I'm also grateful to Scott Matthews, whose sense of humor and energetic support sustained me.

I would especially like to thank the sisters who opened their lives to me and wanted to be included in this volume. Their willingness to discuss the joys and challenges of being sisters made working on *No Friend Like a Sister* one of the most satisfying experiences of my life.

Barbara Alpert

BARBARA ALPERT has worked as a book editor for Bantam, Ballantine, and Avon and as a stage manager for the New York Shakespeare Festival. She is the coauthor of six previous books, including *How to Be a Christmas Angel* (with Scott Matthews) and *HELP: Healthy Exchanges Lifetime Plan* (with JoAnna M. Lund). Her articles have appeared in *Cosmopolitan*, *ParentSource*, *New York Running News*, and other publications. An honors graduate of Brandeis University, she has taught publishing as Adjunct Associate Professor at Hofstra University.